Letters to Lisa

Conversations With a Christian Teacher

Letters to Lisa

Conversations With a Christian Teacher

by John Van Dyk

Dordt Press

Printed in the United States of America.

dp Dordt Press
498 Fourth Avenue NE
Sioux Center, Iowa 51250

ISBN: 0-932914-37-3

doodles, diagrams, and dividers by the author

cover design by Janna Plasier

To my children,
each one of whom contributed in a special way:

Lisa,
whose e-mail messages with questions about how to teach gave me the original idea for *Letters to Lisa*

John K.,
whose computer expertise and text critique were indispensable

Wendy,
whose gifts of language and artistic design have always been impressive

Tricia,
who left school and friends behind for my semester's leave of absence

Letters to Lisa presents important principles for Christian teachers and does so in a delightfully refreshing and readable manner. This book would be a wonderful gift for a college teacher-education graduate.

Gloria Goris Stronks
Calvin College

Letters to Lisa invites you to eavesdrop on the accrued wisdom of a master teacher. Lisa's father tackles the common and crucial issues that face the beginning teacher in an engaging, conversational style. Mentor teachers will find a wealth of insight and younger teachers will gain both comfort and direction.

Andrew White
Christian Parent-Controlled
Schools, Australia

Letters to Lisa indicates that teaching is a complex process requiring decision making on many fronts. The book can be used to stimulate discussions about many basic components of the process of education. It introduces issues from the perspective of a beginning teacher who struggles to give definition to her thinking in interactions with her father. From the father's responses it is obvious that educational practice needs to give expression to a vision. Each letter will likely create stimulating discussions in staff meetings and may lead teachers to re-examine their principles and practices.

John Vanderhoek
Society of Christian Schools
in British Columbia

CONTENTS

PREFACE

To the uninformed, teaching looks like a pretty soft job. What, please tell me, is so backbreaking about strolling into a classroom, herding students into their seats, and getting them to open their books? And what is hard about explaining a lesson here and there, showing a video or two, and putting grades on a report card? Honestly now, teaching is no more strenuous a job than baby sitting, right? A soft touch with long vacations to boot! Beats real work, don't you think?

Even college students preparing for a teaching career commonly entertain such mistaken notions. Some in the elementary track, for example, look forward to endless days of fun and games with innocent, sweet little children. They envision a perpetually jolly good time entertaining little angels with pigtails and freshly scrubbed faces. Prospective high school teachers, meanwhile, dream of the days when they can hold forth on their favorite subject amid spellbound, industrious students. Alas! Reality quickly shatters such dreams. Not long after their first experiences in a real classroom the rookies can be heard to mutter: "Why didn't anyone tell me that teaching would be so hard?"

No doubt some of the idealistic ideas about teaching stem from our personal experience with classrooms. All of us have been with teachers for at least twelve years, and many of us much longer than that. Presumably we know all about education, about schools, and about classrooms. After years of sitting in desks, studying textbooks, taking tests, and following instructions, what is there about teachers and teaching we don't know? The problem is, we acquired this wealth of knowledge while we were students.

We have come to see teaching only from a learner's point of view. And such a point of view rarely perceives what teaching is actually all about. As students we get little sense of how hard, how demanding, how emotionally draining teaching can be. The truth is, unless you teach, you do not know what teaching really is. In one respect, teaching is a wee bit like driving a motorcycle or piloting an airplane: you don't know what it is really like until you actually do it.

It does not take long for the rookie to realize that everything learned in the teacher education program has to be relearned in the day-to-day practice of teaching children. Suddenly all that stuff about philosophy of education, classroom management, child development, learning theories, and lesson planning takes on new and urgent meaning. Suddenly it becomes very clear that there is still so much more to learn.

For a Christian teacher the situation is even more complicated and demanding. A Christian teacher wants not only to teach and teach well, but to teach Christianly, in a way that pleases the Lord. A Christian teacher faces the additional difficulty of having to ask about his or her classroom practice: How do I teach in a Christ-honoring way?

To answer this question requires sustained—and communal—reflection. But reflection takes time, and for teachers time is in short supply. When reflection falls by the wayside, teaching assumes an increasingly pragmatic character. What then comes to guide the teacher is not a sound Christian perspective, continuously sharpened by careful self-evaluation, but a patchwork of short-range solutions to the immediacies of the classroom.

Such pragmatism is a very serious problem. Solutions do not come easily. One way to create time for reflection is to reduce the teaching load by half. But economic reality is not likely to permit such a drastic course of action. Nevertheless, time for reflection, along with appropriate resources, must be provided if Christian teachers are to do their work in a professional, responsible manner.

Letters to Lisa seeks to encourage such reflection. I hope the book will be useful, first of all, to the individual Christian teacher whose passion it is to teach Christianly, whether in a private or public school. I also hope that principals and other educational leaders will look at this book as a potential stimulus for staff discussion and development. In order for this book to be a staff development tool, I have prefaced each letter with a question and I have kept each letter relatively short. Each chapter can be read in a brief span of time.

Letters to Lisa addresses twenty-two common educational, classroom issues, ranging from specific teaching strategies to the question of whether Christians can teach Christianly in a public school. I have sought to treat these questions in a readable, nontechnical style. *Letters to Lisa* is not at all a philosophical treatise. It is a practical book intended to stimulate Christian teachers to reflect on their practice. My desire is two-fold: I've tried to help teachers see that everyday classroom practice is indeed determined by our fundamental beliefs about education and about the Christian life, and to suggest ways of teaching in a biblical way. I say a biblical way because, of course, it would be insufferably arrogant, indeed quite mistaken, to claim that my way is the way. We see but through a glass darkly. Sometimes the glass can be frustratingly opaque.

Lisa is a fifth-grade teacher with two years' experience. She teaches in a Christian school and takes her work very seriously. Lisa loves her students and is deeply interested in their learning. She aims to be a reflective Christian practitioner. Her character and teaching style will become clear as you read the e-mail messages and letters. The issues discussed, however, are not limited to a fifth-grade level. They are common issues that all elementary and high school teachers experience in one way or another. While some letters lend themselves particularly to teachers in a Christian school (such as the letter on devotions), the book as a whole is designed to be useful to Christians teaching in a public school as well.

A word about the tone. The conversations recorded in this book—many of them by e-mail—reflect a dual relationship. On the one hand, the discussions are between two professional educators. At the same time, the two professionals are a father and his daughter. Not surprisingly, then, the letters from Dad occasionally assume a somewhat paternalistic tone. While such paternalism should not be lightly overlooked, it is understandable. On occasion Lisa might rightly remind her father that she is no longer a little girl. Rather, she is a competent, professional teacher, one who is open to advice, but ultimately is equipped to make up her own mind. What both father and daughter have equally in common, however, is their commitment to the task of teaching Christianly.

ACKNOWLEDGMENTS

I want to say thank-you to all the folks who have encouraged me to write this book. Among these are the numerous practicing teachers in the United States, Canada and abroad, who during the past dozen years or so allowed me to enter their classrooms for purposes of observation, collaboration, and pedagogical experimentation. Without the extensive practical experience these teachers provided for me, a book of this sort could easily have turned into an idyllic bit of ivory-tower drivel.

Thanks also to the administrators at Dordt College who approved my request for a semester's leave-of-absence so I could write without distractions. I am also grateful to my colleagues in the Education Department for their unwavering support. I make special mention of Dr. Rick Eigenbrood who willingly took over my teaching assignments, and Dr. Jack Fennema who volunteered to substitute for me as director of the Center for Educational Services.

A special word of thanks to the critical readers who generously took time to evaluate the first draft and offer numerous helpful suggestions:

- Frank De Vries, who recently retired after more than 30 years of experience teaching grades five and six—at Lisa's level.

- Dr. Stuart Fowler, a gifted and widely published Christian philosopher of education, who hosted me at his home in Melbourne, Australia, just to discuss this book.

- Robert Koole, secondary education coordinator of the Society of Christian Schools in British Columbia, experienced in teaching and staff development.

- Dr. Gloria Stronks of Calvin College, a person who knows how teachers think.

- Dr. Harro Van Brummelen of Trinity Western University, himself an author of three books on curricular and instructional theory and practice.

- John Vanderhoek, elementary coordinator of the Society of Christian Schools in British Columbia, whose extensive teaching experience and expertise in elementary education equipped him to provide a detailed critical reading of the first draft.

- Andrew White, an experienced teacher and now one of the directors of Christian Parent-Controlled Schools in Australia.

A special thank-you, as well, to the editor, Kim Rylaarsdam. She meticulously scrutinized the manuscript and made numerous creative suggestions. She helped me walk through the publishing process in a critical yet supportive manner.

Finally, a great big thank-you to my wife Susan. In a sense she co-authored this book. Together we discussed, in detail, the contents of each one of the letters before they were actually put on paper. She took full responsibility for formatting, arranging, and printing the various drafts. She spurred me on when I seemed to grow tired of the project. Though it may sound hackneyed and trite, the fact is that without her this book could not have been prepared.

John Van Dyk, Ph.D.

Center for Educational Services
Dordt College

Spring 1997

1

Teaching Christianly: what is it?

Subject: Advice, please!
From: Lisa
To: Dad
Date: Wed, 6 Sep 16:35:03 -0700 (PDT)

Hi Dad:

Just a quick e-mail message to let you know that I welcome your comments and advice, especially now that the new term has started. It's going to be a challenging year: I've got 27 (do I dare say "rascally"?) kids in my class. But already I love them all—even Keith who seems to be a live wire, to say the least! They're such neat kids! Stephanie is so bubbly—she'll brighten my day. Marci often wears a long face; I'll have to work with her. I tell you, Dad, I'm so eager to teach them! But I worry a bit that I may lose my bearings, so to speak. I mean, I really do want to teach Christianly, as you always tell me I should. But what does that really mean? Isn't it just a cliché? In college I learned a lot of philosophy and theology, but to be honest, all that theory seems miles away from my classroom. Here I am, every day faced with all these fifth-graders, discipline policies, bells and fire drills, piles of bureaucratic administrative stuff, and a schedule that keeps me hopping from morning to night. . . . I've got no time to *think* about teaching Christianly, let alone *do* it! I do open the day with devotions—even have prayer requests—and we sing quite well, thanks to the piano lessons you gave me. But somehow I feel that these efforts are not enough. I'm missing something . . . and right now I just can't put my finger on it. Can you?

Love, Lisa

Subject: Re: Advice, please!
From: Dad
To: Lisa
Date: Wed, 6 Sep 19:00:25 -0500 (CDT)

Dear Lisa,

Thanks for your e-mail message. I want to reply right away—especially now that your new term has just started—because you raise an issue that goes to the heart of what you and I are supposed to be doing. In fact, as Christian teachers, we cannot really talk about teaching without asking, "How do we teach Christianly?" This sort of question, of course, is not limited to Christian teachers. Christian business people, politicians, artists, what have you, also face the same challenge: How do we carry out our task in a way that pleases the Lord? How do we walk with the Holy Spirit in our daily work? Addressing this question will take a bit of time. I'll tell you what: I'll write you a letter this evening and put it in the mail first thing in the morning, okay? Now it's time for supper!

Dad

Wednesday, September 6 9:00 p.m.

Dear Lisa,

I like the way you described the problem in your e-mail message this afternoon. Clearly, you want to take your calling as a Christian teacher seriously. Good for you! Sometimes it happens, I am sorry to say, that Christian teachers are not all that concerned about what it means to teach Christianly. Sometimes they think that there is no such thing as "teaching Christianly," and even parents and school board members sometimes believe that all is well as long as we have church-going Bible-believing Christians teaching in our classrooms.

At other times teachers in Christian schools get tired of the debate about what teaching Christianly really means. You know the issues we squabble about: Should teachers work hard at getting their students to commit themselves to the Lord, or should the emphasis fall on seeing subject matter from a Christian perspective? Are devotions and Bible courses important, or can we do without them? Is it true that as long as a teacher models exemplary Christian behavior everything is hunky-dory? And so on.

Now I realize that we are talking about a complicated and controversial matter. Nevertheless, before we get discouraged and decide to stick our heads in the sand—not an appealing prospect!—let's first ask and answer a fundamental question: Do we believe that Jesus Christ is Lord of *all*? Is he, for you and me, a full-time or a part-time Lord? This question, of course, echoes another one: Are we full-time or part-time Christians? The answer is clear, isn't it? We can't be part-time Christians any more than that we can be part-time husbands or part-time wives. And, as the saying goes, if Christ is not Lord of *all*, he is not Lord at all.

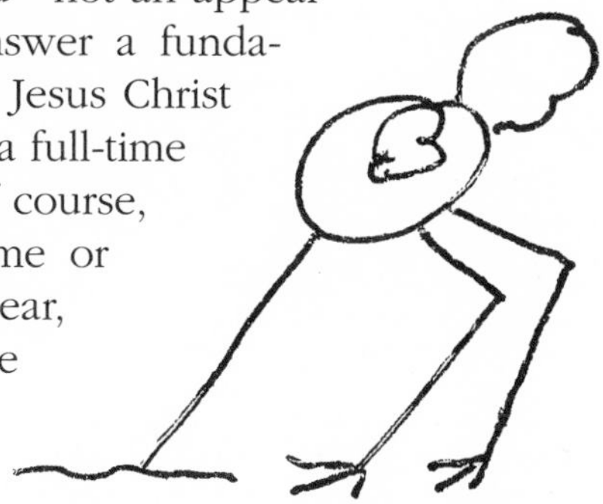

To me this lordship concept means that teaching Christianly is not an optional sort of thing. As Christians we do not have the choice whether or not to teach Christianly, just as I, a married man, do not have the option to be a bachelor once in a while. Of course, I can choose to be unfaithful. But is that really an option? God forbid! So it is with teaching: We can, as Christians, *simply* teach: simply teach our stuff—simply follow the teacher's manual, for example—without any regard for whether or not we teach *Christianly*. But doing so is a form of unfaithfulness, it seems to me. It is, in fact, allowing secularism to enter our classroom. What is secularism? Basically, wherever and whenever I ignore or set aside the will of God, I become secular. I invite such secularism when, for example, I make sure I attend church on Sunday but for the rest of the week pay little attention to how I live my life. So, too, our teaching must be Christian, not just sometimes here and there, but all the time. But now comes your question: Just *how* do we do this?

I suggest you and I begin by asking some soul-searching questions about ourselves as classroom teachers. I am not talking about lesson plans and teaching strategies or evaluation procedures. I'm asking: What kind of people are we in the classroom? How do the students see us? Can they see that we love the Lord and want to live our life in service to Him? You recall the fruit of the Spirit that Paul talks about in Galatians 5. Already in Sunday school, I remember, you learned the list by heart. It contains probably the most basic attributes of a Christian teacher: love, joy, peace, patience, kindness, goodness, faithfulness, gentleness, and self-control. Think about them for a moment, Lisa, and ask yourself: do I display these fruits, or just their opposite? Am I loveless, crabby, impatient, harsh, and short-tempered too often?

I am talking about the old theme of modeling. Yes, I am still old-fashioned enough to believe that teaching Christianly first of all requires good modeling. I can be a competent teacher who knows all the ins and outs of his subject matter and even has an impressive Christian perspective, but if I have not love and patience and the other fruits of the Spirit, my teaching doesn't amount to a bowl of chili beans. I may be teaching the curriculum, even doing an acceptable job, but not teaching *Christianly*. The Apostle Paul makes this point crystal clear in I Corinthians 13.

Of course, to model love and peace and so on is not something we can do on our own. It requires daily repentance and much prayer. Only if we rely on God, totally and unconditionally, can the Spirit of Christ use us as instruments. Only if we recognize that in ourselves we are weak can we be strong in Him. Ultimately, it's God's grace alone that lets us become the sort of models the Lord wants us to be.

Besides modeling the fruit of the Spirit, teaching Christianly requires the right kind of teacher-student relationships. Now this is a huge and complicated subject. Some other time we may want to pursue it in detail. For now, let me just suggest that you carefully check three items: How encouraging are you to the students, what sort of classroom atmosphere do you maintain, and what kind of discipline do you exercise? I know you study the Scriptures, so I know you must have been struck by how often the New Testament admonishes us to encourage each other in the Lord. It is so easy to be negative and hypercritical. It is more difficult to be encouraging, I know! I frequently fall short here. We must encourage our students, Lisa, spurring them on to good works (which includes good learning), just as the Lord encourages us and spurs us on.

And check your classroom atmosphere. Is your classroom a pleasant, happy place in which the students are encouraged to help each other and work together? Or does it resemble a zoo full of wild animals eager to devour one another? Do the children trust you and each other, and do you trust them? Or is your classroom atmosphere choking with fear and suspicion? Lisa, our classrooms should be places where the Holy Spirit loves to be present. On the door should be a sign with huge letters: "Welcome to our class, Holy Spirit!" And when it comes to discipline: Is our main concern simply class management or punishing children for misbehavior in the hope that others will see the folly of such ways? I hope not. Remember that if you *must* exercise discipline—try to prevent having to do so in the first place—it must be done in a loving, *restorative* manner. Discipline must guide students back on track—not easy, especially when it comes to some of those rascally kids, like Keith, who may drive you up the proverbial wall.

So teaching Christianly means modeling, encouragement, a good environment, and restorative discipline? Well, that is surely a big part of it. But there is more. There is, for example, our calling to open up the world to the children. We use our subject matter as keys. At this point the matter of Christian perspective becomes a central theme. Your students must clearly see that we live in God's wonderful creation, that sin has distorted everything, but that Christ came to redeem it all. Read that marvelous first chapter of Colossians again, especially verses 19 and 20. When you teach language or science or social studies or whatever, try to have the students sense something of God's design and intention for the world. Make sure they see how human creatures have twisted and distorted what the Lord meant to be pure and delightful. And teach them how they can be agents of reconciliation, as Paul calls us in II Corinthians 5. You can't dwell on these themes in every lesson, of course. But your units, at the least, should make all of these things unambiguously clear. Christian teachers in public schools will face some severe restraints. Yet there, too, something of this biblical framework should come through.

There is still more. I mean, what is the point of all the teaching you do? The *real* point? To stuff empty heads? To win approval from the sixth-grade teachers? Of course not. In his letter to the Ephesians the Apostle Paul gives us a clue in chapter 4. You have been appointed a teacher to equip students for works of service. This is no drivel! On the contrary, it puts our entire teaching task in context. And it tells us how important it is to create a classroom atmosphere in which the students strive to be of service to each other. You know, it is easy to tell the children how to behave. It's quite another thing to give them opportunities to *practice* how to behave. Once I saw a first-grade teacher work at this. He had just finished with a math activity, and the children had to help each other put the manipulatives away. Some of the youngsters didn't do the task quite right. So the teacher stopped the clean-up midway and said: "Okay, kids, let's take a look at what's happening. What are we doing wrong and how can we do it right?" He asked the children to describe in detail and to model how to do the clean-up and how not to do the clean-up. Then he had them practice several times. All of this took time. It would have been easier and more efficient if he had simply disciplined the troublemakers. But he didn't. He had the students both understand *and* practice active servanthood.

Remember, Lisa, that our classrooms are expressions of the body of Christ. Teaching Christianly involves aggressively seeking to make this a reality. Don't get caught in talking a sweet Christian game, meanwhile fostering individualism and unhealthy competition.

So when you plan your lessons and learning activities, make sure to structure in plenty of opportunity for practicing discipleship and servanthood skills. You have to *work* at this goal. It just doesn't automatically happen. Sin is the big obstacle here. Teaching Christianly requires the keen recognition of sin and a commitment to fight it wherever you see it.

You may remember that on earlier occasions we have described teaching Christianly as guiding, unfolding, and enabling. As guides we nudge the children along—by modeling, encouraging, disciplining, and structuring our classrooms for learning. As teachers and learners we unfold God's creation, and in so doing enable our students to be disciples of the Lord.

Easy? Of course not. Teaching Christianly may well be the hardest job in the universe. But we don't do it alone. We do it together with colleagues, the principal, the parents, the students, and, of course, with the Lord Himself.

Be sure to keep thinking about our calling as Christian teachers, Lisa. Be much in prayer about it as well. Keep talking to your fellow teachers and the principal about it. And, of course, don't hesitate to press me again and again on this issue: teaching Christianly is a topic we can never completely exhaust!

Dad

Subject: Teaching Christianly
From: Lisa
To: Dad
Date: Fri, 8 Sep 17:26:56 -0700 (PDT)

Thanks for the letter, Dad. Nice stuff! But I'm surprised that you haven't said anything about devotions. Is that not part of teaching in a Christian way?

Love, Lisa

Subject: Re: Teaching Christianly
From: Dad
To: Lisa
Date: Fri, 8 Sep 20:07:54 -0500 (CDT)

Dear Lisa,

Yes, devotions are indeed important. But remember that devotional activities by themselves do not a Christian teacher make, just as faithful Sunday church attendance does not guarantee an acceptable Christian lifestyle. If devotions constituted the essential ingredient that makes teaching Christian, then where would Christian teachers in public schools be?

Now in a Christian school, teaching Christianly is well served by good devotions. I think a key issue is how you *perceive* classroom devotions. They so easily become merely a perfunctory ritual: a Bible passage, maybe a devotional reading, a prayer, a song, and we're done. Devotions of this sort often do little to create the kind of mutually serving classroom atmosphere I talked about in my letter. I would like to see teachers use devotions to help the children experience the presence of God. To do so, teachers will have to acknowledge their weakness and to explain frankly that they, in their personal lives, strive to walk arm in arm with the Holy Spirit. They should make plain that in their own lives they want God to walk beside them, not as someone watching to see what they do wrong, but as a loving, supporting, and encouraging father, one who sustains them and urges them onward, who picks them up when they stumble. Christian teachers in public schools, unable to set aside time for explicitly devotional sessions, can nevertheless present themselves as people with weaknesses and failings but whose strength comes from God. They, too, should strive to depict the Lord as their Heavenly Father who walks along with them.

Ideally, devotional activities should involve a gathering around the Scripture to be instructed by God's Word. There should be plenty of opportunity for responses. Especially important will be to hear the Word of God speak not only to our lives as individuals, but to our *life together in the classroom*. In this way devotions set a tone for the day and pervade all the other classroom activities we design. I make this point only in passing. At a later date we might spend more time exploring the nature and role of devotional activities in our classrooms.

As ever, Dad

2

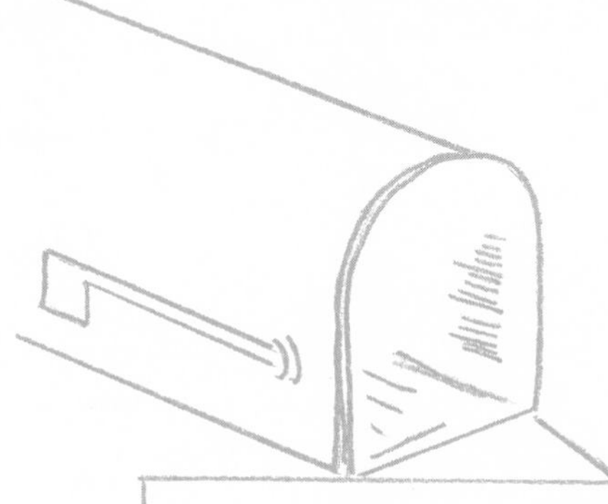

What learning objectives should I write in my lesson and unit plans?

Subject: Learning objectives
From: Lisa
To: Dad
Date: Thu, 14 Sep 18:35:17 -0700 (PDT)

Hi Dad,

Sorry for troubling you with a phone call earlier today. But I was really upset! Now that I've simmered down, I can look at the situation more objectively. Here's what happened:

Our principal called a special staff meeting this afternoon—even invited a few members of the education committee—and announced a new approach to lesson planning. "We're turning over a new leaf," he declared. "We're going to put a new emphasis on lesson planning, goals and objectives, and outcomes. We have to have a clearer view of what we're trying to do in our classrooms." He went on to make it abundantly clear that from now on he wants us to pay special attention to writing carefully formulated *performance* objectives. He did not go so far as to commit our school to outcome-based education. In fact, I think he rejects outcome-based education as an unchristian idea.

Believe me, Dad, I wasn't the only one who was upset: our entire staff felt hurt because of what looked to us like unfair criticism. To us his message meant: "You dummies don't *really* know what you're doing or where you are going! You don't have a clue! Quit shooting into the air and start aiming for some concrete targets!" Quite frankly, Dad, we felt insulted. Look, we may not always be thinking deep thoughts about goals and objectives, but we're pretty competent people. We have a pretty good idea of what we want our kids to learn and a pretty good idea of how to get the job done. We don't believe that "turning over a new leaf" and having to write all sorts of fancy objectives is going to make any real difference in how we teach. What do you think, Dad? Is this performance objectives stuff really going to help us teach more effectively, more

Christianly? Or will it make an already tough job even more difficult? Think of all the extra paperwork!

Zip me back a reply, okay? Thanks!

Love, Lisa

Subject: Re: Learning objectives
From: Dad
To: Lisa
Date: Thu, 14 Sep 21:15:23 -0500 (CDT)

Dear Lisa,

Thanks for the e-mail. I keenly sense your feelings of frustration and hurt. Let me ask you a question: Could it be that the principal might have the best in mind for your school? I doubt that he is implementing these new expectations as a form of criticism or torture. You yourself have frequently commented on his strong commitment to Christian education. Besides, let's be clear: lesson planning, goals and objectives, and all that sort of stuff *is* important. Once we begin to neglect the planning phase we will soon be drifting along and lose our professionalism.

Because of time limitations and other pressures, teachers often skimp in their planning and are forced to be satisfied with generalities such as "today I'll cover pp. 35-42 in the social studies text," or "I think I'll have the kids write a few essays," or "If only I can keep Shelley in line, I'll make it through the day!" Such goals say nothing about what you want the students to learn or experience, and so you may end up, as you heard your principal put it, "shooting in the air with no targets in sight."

Or, on the other hand, when teachers do not pay explicit attention to learning goals, they easily become myopic, focusing on some learning objectives and ignoring others. For example, they may concentrate on content, on facts, or on skills and might forget that their units and lessons are to aim for the largest learning goal of all: to equip our students for knowledgeable and competent discipleship. So, yes, I think writing objectives represents an important aspect of teaching Christianly. Give it a fresh look, okay?

Dad

Subject: Re: Learning objectives
From: Lisa
To: Dad
Date: Thu, 14 Sep 19:45:32 -0700 (PDT)

Hi Dad,

I just got your note. You did not really answer my question. I asked specifically about *performance objectives*. I always thought performance objectives were inspired by behaviorism, and surely behaviorism is a philosophy we should avoid, right? I thought you were sort of down on behaviorism! By the way, by "performance objectives" I mean—and I think our principal means—*measurable* objectives that state exactly what a kid will be able to do after one of our lessons. Do you really believe we should be asked to spend eons of our precious time writing and planning for such objectives? You can't be serious!

Love, Lisa

Subject: Re: Learning objectives
From: Dad
To: Lisa
Date: Thu, 14 Sep 22:15:43 -0500 (CDT)

Dear Lisa,

Sorry I missed the point of your earlier question. Let me try to do better. Yes, I think you have defined a performance objective correctly. Such objectives are stated with precision and lend themselves to accurate assessment. For my science lesson, for example, I could write a performance objective such as this: "Given the textbook's treatment of reptiles and amphibians, the students will be able to distinguish between a lizard and a salamander by stating three different characteristics of each." This objective clearly articulates what I want the students to learn, and the learning will be easy to measure.

I do think, Lisa, that such objectives, though cumbersome and time-consuming to write out, are okay for certain types of lessons. They are useful for situations where it is important for you to know whether or not your students have mastered specific content or skills. But if these kinds of objectives become the rule, watch out! Then we are in danger of miring ourselves in the murky swamps of behaviorism, as you already suggested. We will then assume that real learning occurs only when students can exemplify, in a measurable way, a specific change in behavior. If they can state, for example, the three differences between lizards and salamanders, and if I can objectively assess their statements, I presumably know that they have grasped the difference between these two types of creatures, and that real learning has occurred. I think you sense, Lisa, the very narrow understanding of knowledge and learning implied in this approach. Yet this kind of behaviorism can still be found in all sorts of schools. In elementary schools, for example, it is reflected in the continual measuring of basic skills, in high

Subject: Re: Learning Objectives
From: Lisa
To: Dad
Date: Fri, 15 Sep 15:33:21 -0700 (PDT)

Hi Dad,

Thanks for your comments about performance objectives. I'll have to think about them some more. But if performance is one type of objective, and expressive objectives are different, what sort of outcomes should expressive objectives aim for? You know what I'm asking, don't you?

Love, Lisa

Subject: Re: Learning Objectives
From: Dad
To: Lisa
Date: Fri, 15 Sep 20:17:31 -0500 (CDT)

Dear Lisa,

You ask an important question. Instead of harping on performance objectives, let me put the issue more positively: What learning goals should we Christian teachers aim for? Bloom's taxonomy might give us one clue. He suggests three domains of learning goals: cognitive, affective and psychomotor. But be careful: Bloom's taxonomy distinguishes too sharply between "cognitive" and "affective" domains. By the "affective domain" he means such things as feelings, beliefs, and attitudes. I don't like this term "affective," Lisa, and I equally dislike the implication that somehow we can bottle up feelings and beliefs and attitudes into a distinct domain. The fact is, there *is* no knowledge without belief and feeling, and there *are* no beliefs and feelings and attitudes without knowledge. All knowledge is colored by what we believe and how we feel.

As an alternative to Bloom, let me suggest at least six general areas of learning objectives. Each one of these areas should be addressed somewhere in your unit plan. Some will require more emphasis, depending a bit on the subject matter, but none may be disregarded or neglected. These "goal areas" should not be viewed as separate unrelated categories: they overlap and interact. Most importantly, each one of these goal areas should contribute to the overarching goal of equipping for discipleship.

The first of these areas concerns the learning of contents and skills, the sort of thing most lesson objectives are about. If you want to write performance objectives, I suspect most of them would fit in this category.

Second, I suggest you pay special attention to developing the children's capacity to think critically. I know this emphasis is getting to be a fad nowadays, but we need to remember that we want our youngsters to be able to distinguish sharply and evaluate soundly.

A third category of learning objectives should aim at the children's creative and imaginative abilities. Too often, I fear, the creativity of our youngsters is thought to be the responsibility of art and music teachers. Not so, of course. Every teacher, no matter what the subject, should provide plenty of opportunity for the exercise of creativity and imagination. Creative writing, drama, improvisation, sketching, composing, and the like are appropriate to virtually any lesson you may wish to teach. In fact, I suspect that every part of the curriculum can be dramatized or turned into a creative activity.

The fourth goal area may remind you of the old "psychomotor domain" of Benjamin Bloom. It has to do with physical, hands-on learning. We can easily get stuck in classroom routines of seatwork and cerebral labor. So we must think of ways to engage the children in concrete, physical activity. Don't leave this job entirely to the P.E. teachers. Manipulatives in math are an excellent beginning. Some of the creative activities suggested above lend themselves to bodily actions. And don't hesitate to get the children involved in hands-on learning. Look for opportunities to have them construct and build, to forge and to assemble. From what you've said, Keith might be a prime candidate for this goal area.

A fifth set of learning objectives focuses on the social and emotional development of your children. For Marci such goals may be much more important than academic skills. Marci needs to develop a positive attitude towards herself and others. These are relevant emotional and social objectives. At times it will be important to teach your students to express righteous anger. In social studies and science, for example, it is not enough to simply have the youngsters understand the breakdown of the family and the effects of air pollution. They should be upset about such evils and want to do something about them. We are talking about direct consequences of sin, and sin is something to be angry about! The Lord certainly is!

I suggest, Lisa, that a key emotional goal should be that your students will *enjoy* your class. I mean genuine enjoyment and satisfaction from meaningful learning, not superficial entertainment. If you write at the top of your lesson plan—"The students will enjoy this lesson" you will be motivated to teach in more creative ways, I'm sure. Now is this a measurable performance objective? Of course not. But you surely can tell whether the students are bored to tears or having a good time learning.

A final, very important category of learning objectives focuses on servanthood skills. Again, hard to measure, but not so hard to judge. Be sure to give students like Stephanie, who are a joy to teach, many opportunities and incentives to help Marci and others like her. Teach them to encourage each other, to listen to each other, to respect each other, to pray for each other, and to really love one another.

Meanwhile, you are faced with the principal's decision to focus on performance objectives. What should you do? I would take the following steps: Talk to the principal, and colleagues as well, about some of the themes we have just discussed. Ask him how he can help you maintain your commitment to the *whole* child. Don't argue about performance objectives. Agree to abide by his decision, comply with his requirements, then try to meet other goals as well. Remember, patience and gentleness are two important fruits of the Spirit. Keep me posted, okay?

As always, Dad

3

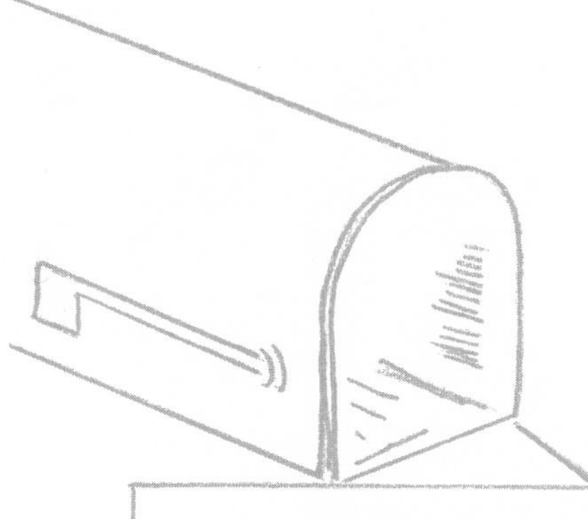

How important is academic excellence as a goal of Christian teaching?

Subject: Seminar
From: Lisa
To: Dad
Date: Sat, 7 Oct 17:16:58 -0700 (PDT)

Hi Dad,

I just got back from an inservice seminar on cognitive development. The workshop leader at the seminar convinced some of my colleagues that schools are, after all, for the training of minds. We had quite a debate in the van on the way back! Alex and Clare, for example, are now gung-ho. They can't wait to get back to their classrooms to implement Bloom's taxonomy of higher-order thinking and what not. Fired up, they are ready to turn the whole curriculum into a model of academic rigor. But Sandy and Jim objected quite vigorously. "That's *not* what our Christian schools are all about. We want to teach in a school where everything revolves around love and caring and things like that!" That's the way I see it too, Dad. Think of Jeffrey in my class! Hardly an academic hair on his head, and yet what a lovely kid! What good would it do to toss Bloom's taxonomy at him? It might ruin him for life! Sandy and Jim and I were together on this point, but the others merely laughed and said, "With logic like that, you yourself could stand some training in critical thinking!"

What do you think, Dad? How does academic excellence fit into this teaching Christianly thing?

Love, Lisa

Saturday, October 7

Dear Lisa,

The way you described the argument, Lisa, makes me suspect that your side may have been firing away with the same kind of ammunition as the opposition, except that you were aiming at different targets: *they* want academic excellence and critical thinking; *you* want discipleship and Christian virtue. I take it the principal was not riding in the van with you. No doubt he would have toned all of you down, don't you think? Isn't he the guy who always talks about the *twin* goals of your school: to be academically the best and to be morally the best? "Our school," he says, "must graduate students who are *both* smart *and* good; youngsters who know what's what and who do the right thing." Might putting it this way not be a reasonable compromise?

I don't blame you for getting a bit hot under the collar, Lisa. The issue you debated with your friends is sufficiently important to merit a bit of steam. Suppose that your school would officially adopt an academic-rigor/excellence-above-all position. Many schools do this, you know. Once I spoke at a large Christian school about the aim of Christian education. Just before my speech the president of the school board gave a little pep talk: "Our school exists in order to give parents a choice between *quality* education and the mickey-mouse fuzzies offered by the public school around the corner." He made it clear that by quality education he meant hard-core academics. Between you and me, I felt a bit like a sheep among wolves.

Mind you, my quibble is not with those who promote excellence. Of course not. We should strive for excellence in all that we do. Schooling requires us to do our best. I do not advocate laziness and sloppiness. My dispute is with those who see *academic* excellence as the *pivotal* goal of Christian teaching.

Suppose *your* school would take a similar stance. What would you do with Jeffrey? What would happen to the child? As you explained in the van, Jeffrey is a lovely, sensitive, kind-hearted youngster, but lousy at grammar and math. Good at drawing pictures of birds, maybe, but somehow academically deficient. So what are you going to do? It would appear that you have only two options: either you do the best you can and let Jeffrey slide by with a D+ for achievement (an A for effort to cheer him up, of course), or you simply toss in the towel and give him a failing grade.

But wait a minute—you have a third option: That is to recognize Jeffrey's limitations and work hard on developing his other gifts. (How to do that we'll talk about another time.) Now a true-blue academic-excellence philosophy probably would not allow you to exercise this third option. In a school in which harsh academic rigor, disguised as "quality education," is the watchword, Jeffrey has no place. Jeffrey will have to settle for less than "the best." Jeffrey cannot benefit from the wonderful, caring, and Christian atmosphere in your classroom. He will have to go to some vocational-technical school where there may be little concern about teaching Christianly.

I do not want to sound judgmental, Lisa, but I do believe that those who worship academic excellence have actually bowed down before an ancient idol, the idol of intellectualism. And what an idol it is! From your philosophy of education classes you may recall some of its shapes: sometimes it goes by the name of rationalism or positivism or perennialism, and the like. Please, Lisa, don't succumb to intellectualism! For all its gloss, it is really a sinister philosophy. It is no good on at least two counts: first, it sweet-talks you into believing that only academic stuff is worthwhile and everything else is second class. You know of schools that see music, art, physical education and industrial programs as frills, and are quick to chuck them when there is a financial crunch. Academic stuff *is* important, but so are the arts and music and P.E. and drama and human feelings and relationships. Being able to get along with your neighbor is just as important as knowing the multiplication tables—yes, more important, if I read the Scriptures correctly!

Secondly, intellectualism tries to make you believe that what makes people human is their rational mind. This is an old pagan belief: train the mind and you train the person. But that slogan isn't true. The Bible gives us a different picture: "Guard your *heart,*" we read in Proverbs 4, "for it is the wellspring of life." Our thoughts come out of our heart, Jesus tells us in Matthew 15. Our supposed "rational mind" is actually supervised and directed by a deeper core of our being. The Scriptures describe this deeper core as the heart or the soul. It determines who we are and what we think. So Christian education should not just be "mind" education, but "heart" education. Don't let intellectualism fool you!

Interestingly, Lisa, current educational and philosophical theories debunk the ancient Greek idea that the "mind" is something rational and academic. Howard Gardner, for example, speaks of "multiple intelligences" and describes many ways—including non-academic—of being "smart." We are wise to follow these discussions closely.

Okay, you say, so our principal has it straight after all: peaceful coexistence, right? Make sure you stress the "rational mind," the academic stuff, the critical thinking and all, but put equal emphasis on the "heart," right? Wrong! Reasonable though it sounds, the coexistence proposal will get you into a pack of trouble. You see, putting it that way invites two independent, even contradictory philosophies to dwell under a single Christian roof: academic excellence plus Christian virtue. The coexistence approach encourages pagan intellectualism to share a bed with a Christian philosophy of education. They will forever contend with each other, each seeking to eke out the larger area for itself. It will lead to the sorts of gun-slinging you folks were doing in the van. No, Lisa, coexistence is a risky proposition.

So what is the answer? Well, consider these steps: First, acknowledge that academics, critical thinking, and Bloom's cognitive taxonomy *are* important and may not be neglected. Don't let anybody talk you into believing that basic knowledge and skills can be slighted or ignored. Next, be sure to ask *the* critical question at this point: *why* is this academic stuff important? So that we can outshine the public school around the corner, as that board president thought? Or see a lot of our students on the honor roll so that our school will look great in the local newspaper? To ferry students on to college and beyond, eventually to make the big bucks (schools generally like alumni with big bucks)? Rubbish! Remember the ultimate goal of the Christian school: to equip young people for works of service. That inevitably involves the "heart" and "mind" and everything else. It embraces the whole person. To be a servant of God in our troubled and complicated world requires the development of *all* of the gifts of *all* our children, not just the academic gifts of a few.

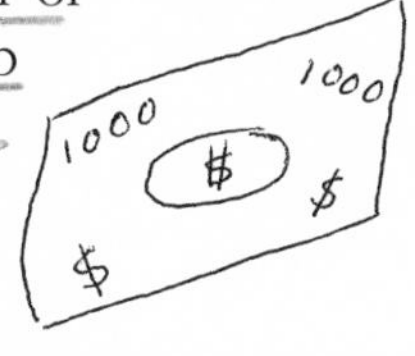

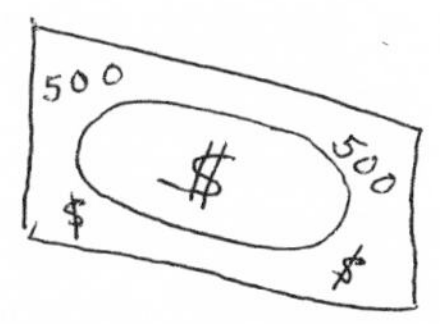

It is your job as a Christian teacher, Lisa, to equip youngsters like Jeffrey for service. But the academic program may not offer the best way to develop his potential. It certainly is not the only way. Jeffrey, I suspect, has many other talents which he can develop for service. And how many other Jeffreys are there in your school? Academic excellence will take them only so far.

So what is the conclusion? I urge you, Lisa, to look at academics as *one* of the avenues to equip for service. It is an important avenue, but it's not the only one. So think back to the seminar on cognitive development you and your colleagues just attended. Pick up as much as you can from people who know about such things. Do not pooh-pooh their insights. But don't get side-tracked by the illusion that now you've found the key to education.
Instead, keep the big picture in view!
And don't forget about Jeffrey!

Happy teaching.

Dad

4

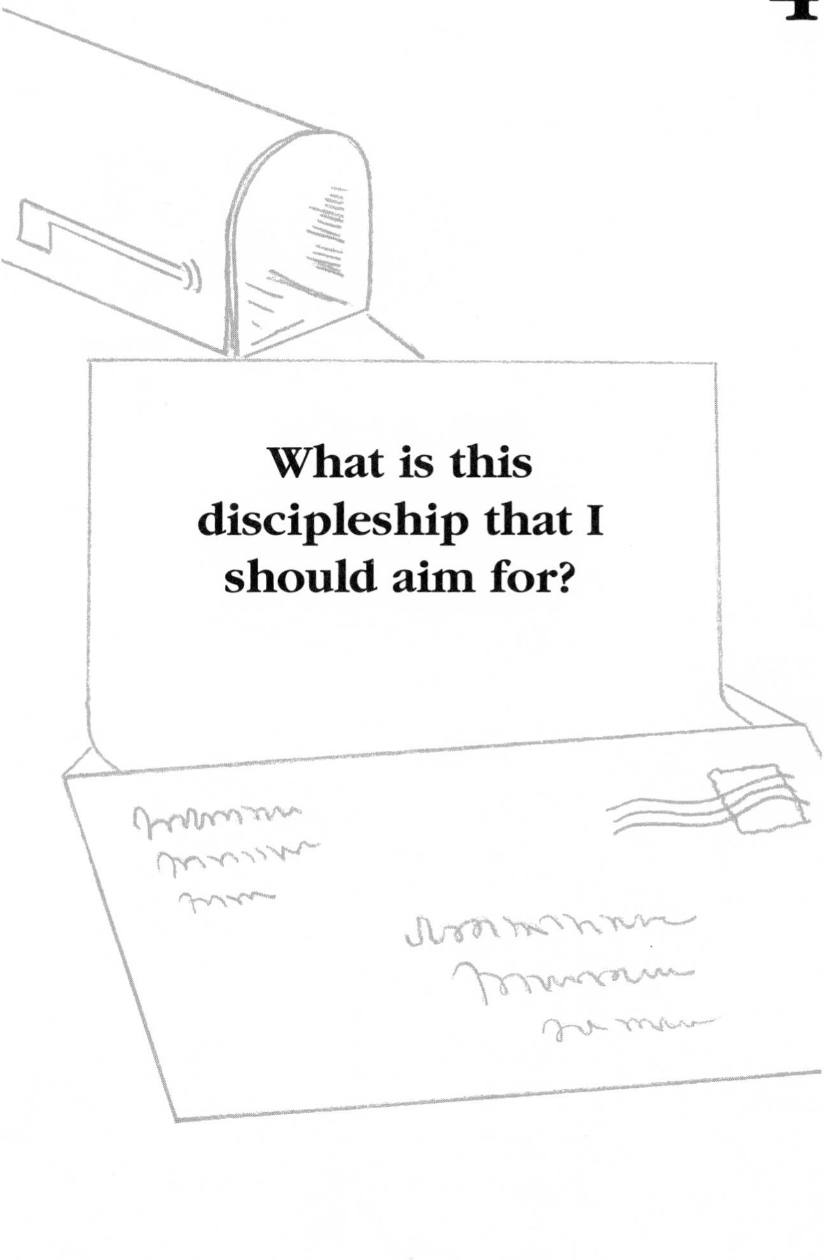

What is this discipleship that I should aim for?

can we identify authentic discipleship? When is it the real thing?

I really think you need to say more about this discipleship thing, Dad. I know you're busy, but I hope you can find time to help me sort out my thoughts on this subject. I'd appreciate it.

Love,

Lisa

Tuesday, October 17

Dear Lisa,

Thanks for your letter. The topic you raise is so big that I don't know whether or not I can adequately address your concerns. Besides, to be honest, I'm not always sure I myself understand completely the ins and outs of discipleship. Discipleship is a rich, inexhaustible concept. We can talk about it for years and never fully take hold of what it means or what it implies. At the same time, I continue to hang on to the idea that discipleship is what life—and teaching Christianly—is all about. We either strive for discipleship or we get stuck in idolatry. Not that we can simply choose to be disciples and presto! our life is in order. Think of Paul who struggled to be a disciple and yet continually fell short. One moment he claims that he can do all things in Christ, while the next he despairs of reaching the high goal of his calling.

While it is hard to fully grasp the meaning of Christian discipleship, it is not so difficult to detect some common misunderstandings. I think we're in trouble and off-track when, for example, we equate discipleship with being a missionary or church worker, or with making a profession of faith, or with accepting a set of doctrines taught by the church. Wearing a "Jesus loves me" button or displaying a "Honk if you love Jesus" bumper sticker is not necessarily evidence of discipleship either. True, such actions may suggest, but they do not define, discipleship.

Sometimes it's easy to get children to accept this sort of superficial discipleship. Think of some of the children in your own class who dutifully bow their heads and close their eyes during devotions, ostensibly signifying discipleship. Overt actions like these or like those I mentioned above may actually mislead us into thinking that true discipleship has been achieved. So the problem you raise is a real one: How can we distinguish between gold and fool's gold? How can we tell genuine discipleship from what may actually be only externals and show?

Let me complicate the issue further: If we describe discipleship as servanthood—as indeed I like to do, as you noted in your letter—then it looks as if we see many "disciples," even though they may not confess Christ as Savior. There are plenty of people who serve. They do the will of the Lord without acknowledging him. Think of all the humanitarian activities, charities, Red Cross missions, social services, and the like; or think of a whole community rallying to help when there is a disaster or a need. Remember when that DC-10 jetliner crashed at the Sioux City airport, killing more than a hundred people? The way the entire city came out to help was news for many weeks. What a splendid exhibition of caring discipleship, right? Often various secular agencies do in the name of social welfare what Christians should be doing in the name of Christ. Some people ask, "Why do we need the church when there is already so much helpfulness in the world?"

In Christian schools, too, we find students who deny Christ and yet are nice kids. I remember one very intelligent young man in my tenth-grade English class who wrote a paper titled, "Why I am not a Christian." In eloquent language he explained his feelings. "I know so much about God," he wrote, "that I hate Him!" Yet he was in most respects what we would call a "nice boy." Similarly, in public schools you find many teachers and students who are not Christian, yet are caring, loving people who live a disciplined life style that might put a Christian school to shame. One friend said to me once: "Why should I send my kids to the Christian school? It costs a lot of money, and I don't see all that much difference between graduates from a Christian and from a public school!"

What shall we say about all of this, Lisa? One thing seems clear: Discipleship is not a clear-cut, easily identified sort of thing. I think of Jesus' story about those who cry, "Lord, Lord, did we not cast out demons?" *et cetera*, and yet are not welcomed into the eternal Kingdom of God. It looks, then, as if discipleship is rife with paradox: Sometimes nonchristians seem to exemplify more genuine discipleship than some Christians do. So does all this confusion suggest that discipleship as an overarching educational goal is nothing but a bunch of impractical balderdash?

Discipleship as an educational goal, Lisa, requires a vision of God's Kingdom, the place where we are to function as channels for his renewing power. By "place" I mean, of course, the entire creation. "The earth is the Lord's and the fullness thereof," the Psalmist declares and Paul reaffirms. Psalm 145 describes the Lord as the great King of the universe. The Kingdom of God, then, is God's good creation, distorted by sin to be sure, but now in a stage of renewal. The Spirit is at work in a fallen world, in the process of making all things new, on the way towards making the Kingdom visible once again. To be a disciple, I think, is to participate in this renewing and redeeming work. Originally we were all disciples—fully human, created for our peculiarly human task of "dressing and keeping the garden," as an earlier translation of Genesis 2 puts it. We were called to unfold God's creation and to take good care of it. So we might say, 100% discipleship is equivalent to doing what humans were created to do in the world, to God's glory.

But sin tarnishes our humanity, and impairs our functioning as disciples. Yet we see traces of true, original discipleship come through, even in sinful situations, just as, conversely, you see discipleship distorted and suppressed in otherwise appropriate, Christ-honoring situations.

What does this mean for you and me as Christian teachers? Well, for one thing, to teach Christianly means, in part, to recognize the original, authentic, serving discipleship according to the intent of God. Teaching Christianly, then, means to equip students for service, even if such service will always be tainted by sin.

This represents a difficult problem, one that has a long tradition of debate and controversy. It is very difficult to understand how sin and redemption can coexist side by side, even within the same person. Think of the parable of the wheat and the tares, or of Paul, who does what he doesn't want to do and the reverse. Think also of Christ's command: Judge not, lest you be judged! Augustine wrestled with the problem in his *City of God*.

The great danger is that we will call all humanistic humanitarian activity—including laudable acts of stewardship and healing—"discipleship," for then we are right back in social gospelism again. Yet it is also dangerous not to recognize the traces of discipleship in such humanitarianism. Wherever the will of God is done, even by unbelievers, there is reason for rejoicing. Such rejoicing should be accompanied by the call for recognition of Christ as Redeemer and King of creation, the real, bottom-line giver of all good things, of life itself.

However we may wish to describe it, discipleship is clearly a matter of action, not of empty words. I worry not so much about youngsters who don't pray or express overtly a love for God—kids who don't appear to be "Christian"—as about those children who are selfish, aggressive, and mean, no matter what they profess. Ultimately, it's by the fruit that we can tell a true disciple—not by what they say, but by what they do.

I am not suggesting that words are unimportant. A true disciple will affirm, in spoken words too, his or her love for the Lord. Speaking, remember, is itself a form of doing. Speaking, believing, thinking—all human activity is to be an expression of loving service to God and neighbor. An all-embracing discipleship will always be curtailed if it does not include a personal attachment to Christ and a reliance on the saving work of Jesus.

Servanthood, stewardship, and peacemaking can ultimately never be discipleship in the full sense of the word if it bypasses faith, repentance, and gratitude. Discipleship in the full, restored sense of the word implies explicitly following Jesus Christ.

Let us not forget that discipleship is a dynamic interaction between hearing and doing. You summarized the model I work with quite well: A disciple is one who *hears* the Word of God and *does* it. Such "doing" has two sides: caretaking and healing. The problem with much of the so-called discipleship is that it consists of doing without the hearing, or of hearing without the doing.

Discipleship = hearing → will of God
↕
doing
stewardship healing

Non-Christians often *do* but do not *hear*. Sin has impaired, even shut down, their hearing. They engage in works of service, but not in response to the Word of the Lord. Or, yes, it *is* a hearing of the will of God—after all, God's voice is heard by everyone, as Psalm 19 and Romans 1 and 2 point out—but it is only a faint hearing, distorted by all sorts of other secularized, humanistic "words," such as "the social good" or "philanthropy" or "humanitarianism." All these are "words" that people hear—words as faint echoes of God's Word—that lead them to do good deeds.

Christians, on the other hand, often *hear* without the *doing*. We *know* the will of God, but do not *act* on our knowledge. We hear God calling us, but respond only with lip-service.

Christian teaching, therefore, has to aim at both hearing and doing. The doing should be attuned to the hearing, and the hearing should lead to the right sort of doing. Christian views of fruit-bearing focus on servanthood in the name of Christ. So the ultimate goal of teaching Christianly cannot be head knowledge or A's on a report card. The ultimate goal is to live, in both word and deed, according to the intentions of God.

Reading over this letter, Lisa, I recognize I've rambled a bit. I'm not sure whether I have clarified anything at all. Maybe you are now more confused than ever. But now that I've written the letter, I'll put it in an envelope, stick a stamp on it, and mail it off. When you come home for Christmas, we might light the fire and continue the conversation. Agreed?

Dad

Subject: Discipleship
From: Lisa
To: Dad
Date: Thu, 19 Oct 09:54:13 -0700 (PDT)

Hi Dad,

Thanks for your letter. Yes, I think it rambles a bit, but I can make some sense of it. I do realize that it's difficult to talk in an organized way about a somewhat abstract topic. What I need is for you to get practical. Here's my question: Can Christian teaching really enable our kids to "hear" and "do"? Remember, you can lead a horse to water, but you can't make it drink! Right?

Love, Lisa

Subject: Re: Discipleship
From: Dad
To: Lisa
Date: Thu, 19 Oct 12:17:21 -0500 (CDT)

Dear Lisa,

Yes, you're right. Although Christian teaching seeks to enable for an all-embracing discipleship, you and I know that it is not we who can really accomplish such a daunting task. Ultimately it is the work of the Lord. As Paul suggests in I Corinthians 3, someone plants, another waters, but God gives the increase. Yes, it has indeed been said that we can lead a horse to water but cannot make it drink. Remember, though, that we can make the horse mighty thirsty! We can feed it salt or make it run around the well until it is ready to drink. So we Christian teachers should do everything we can to make our classrooms the sort of places where our students can and will drink the water of life. We must create the conditions that allow the Holy Spirit to do his enabling work. We recently reviewed some of these conditions, Lisa, when we explored what it means to teach Christianly. I fear that sometimes our classrooms can be depressing places, places filled with fear or self-seeking competition or lovelessness, places where the Spirit is not really welcome and so cannot do his work.

Discipleship is a complicated concept. However we may describe it, and however we may wish to assess it, discipleship surely *is* and *remains* the goal! Achieving it we leave in the hands of the Lord. Don't neglect, meanwhile, to count on the power of prayer!

As ever, Dad

5

Do I teach subjects or students?

Subject: Special committee
From: Lisa
To: Dad
Date: Thu, 19 Oct 15:50:56 -0700 (PDT)

Hi Dad,

Guess what! The principal asked me to chair a committee! He even called it a "task force," so it must be important. :) What he has asked us to do is to come up with a statement on whether our school system—K through 12—should adopt a student-centered or a subject-centered approach to education. The reason for the committee, as far as I know, is that a sizable segment of the constituency has recently put pressure on the principal to make some sort of decision on this matter. Some parents are worried about newfangled educational ideas that coddle and spoil the kids. Especially parents with students in the high school clamor to make our school an explicitly subject-centered enterprise. The parents of children in the elementary school are not quite so vocal, at least, not yet. But recently I read some reports about the pressure put on pre-schools to become more academic, and when I listen to the bellowing about the basics, I think I can make some accurate predictions, don't you agree?

Anyway, I think it's kind of dumb to have to make a choice between subjects and students, so dumb that I don't know whether or not to accept the appointment. If I do, I'd probably try to steer the committee into the direction of a compromise of some sort. We have to pay attention to both subject matter and the kids! If you have any thoughts on the matter—you probably do!—you might share them with me whenever it's convenient to you.

Love, Lisa

Subject: Re: Special Committee
From: Dad
To: Lisa
Date: Thu, 19 Oct 19:12:06 -0500 (CDT)

Dear Lisa,

Just a quick e-mail response. You're absolutely right! You are being asked to respond to a totally illegitimate dilemma. It is absurd, Lisa, to be squished into a position where you have no choice but to choose between a so-called subject-oriented and a student-centered education. Such a choice makes as much sense as having to choose between flour and sugar when making a cake.

Since you teach fifth grade, I suspect you are somewhat caught in the middle, aren't you? I suppose this is part of the reason why the principal asked you to chair a committee mandated to come up with a statement on the matter. The primary reason for the request is, of course, that you have proven yourself to be a "reflective practitioner," insightful and articulate. Whatever the principal's motives, Lisa, I encourage you to accept the invitation. If you have the time for this kind of work, why not give it a shot? It gives you an opportunity to be a positive and healing influence. To encourage you to take the job and start you thinking about it, I will write some comments about this subject-vs.-student argument and mail them to you tomorrow morning, okay?

Dad

Thursday evening, October 19

Dear Lisa,

As you and I and just about everyone else know, the debate about subjects vs. students has a long, though not always illustrious, history. For centuries there was little concern about "student-centered learning." Schooling mostly revolved around subjects, around curricular content. Only a few mavericks like Pestalozzi and Montessori asked long-ignored questions about those on whom we foist all this subject matter.

Only in our own century did student-centered education emerge as a real challenge to traditional schooling. No doubt the decline of rationalism, which stressed universal structures of knowledge, had something to do with this rival approach. The progressivist movement seriously questioned the legitimacy of teaching curriculum without considering how children learn. Well, you know about the progressivists and how they fared. For a while they flourished, then lost steam when they became identified with the failures of the open classroom. A vigorous reaction was not long in coming: what our schools should be all about, the reactionaries declared, is instruction in subject matter and skills. Forget about the progressivist's idealistic picture of children learning naturally in uncontrolled classrooms! Many Christians, conservative at heart, soon felt at home with this perennialist-essentialist orientation. They joined the back-to-the-basics movement and called for renewed attention to a hard-core curriculum, dismissing lingering progressivist protests as "warm fuzzies."

What do we observe here, Lisa? We see Christian educators getting stuck in one of the many pendulum swings that have characterized so much of the history of schooling. The pendulum has swung, and continues to swing, between recurring polarities, such as subjects vs. students, core curriculum vs. electives, direct instruction vs. cooperative learning, phonics vs. whole language, content vs. process, exclusion vs. inclusion, tracking vs. heterogeneous grouping, and on and on. It is peculiar but true that Christians seldom ask where these polarities originated in the first place; instead, we tend to join one side or another without asking fundamental questions.

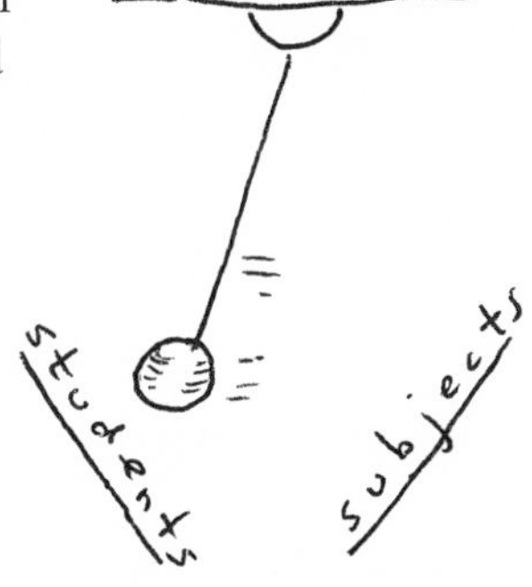

Before you impatiently ask me what all of these ruminations have to do with your assignment, let me add a footnote to this pendulum situation. It has to do with fads. You know all about fads, right? Education is full of them. Their abundance is one reason why change in education—including change for the better—is so difficult to get going: new ideas and approaches are quickly and easily dismissed as "fads."

Now, to be sure, there have been plenty of worthless fads. But there are examples of "good fads" as well, fads that were originally viewed with suspicion but over time gained a rightful place in the educational arena. Think, for example, of the history of Black education or the introduction of psychology into teacher education. These were once fads. Now they are permanent fixtures, as natural as a shoe store in a mall.

My point is this: All this pendulum and polarization business is excellent grist for the fad mill. For a fad has at least two characteristics: First, it is always a reductionism, that is, it thinks that what it is proposing is the only right way and all that is needed. In so doing a fad dismisses other options. Whole language, for example, becomes a fad when its supporters believe that it is the only way to learn to read. Cooperative learning becomes a fad when its proponents say it is the panacea for all of our educational ills. This situation points to the second characteristic of a fad: we load it down with unreasonable and unrealistic expectations. Take progressivism, for example. Not only was the movement reductionistic, declaring all other educational approaches to be hopelessly outmoded and irrelevant, but also presumed that with progressivism education had reached its "grand finale," the point of perfection.

You see then, Lisa, that when we Christians get caught up in these reductionistic polarities, we are setting ourselves up for a fad, and, consequently, for the disappointment that will inevitably follow. I encourage you to try to make this clear in your report.

Okay, you say, so what can we do? Use an ostrich approach and pretend that there are no choices? Well, yes, we could do that. That response in itself would be a choice. My argument is that taking a position for or against subject-centered or student-centered education will lock you into a reductionistic, faddish pendulum swing.

What about a middle way, you ask? And, yes, within Christian educational circles there have been attempts to have it both ways: We need *both* subject-centered *and* student-centered education, it has been proposed. Take the two choices and slap them together. Now surely such an approach is better than opting for either one. Putting them together certainly recognizes that somehow both are necessary.

But be careful, Lisa! Simply constructing a compromise between the two leaves us with a fundamental problem. We are still left with the tension: Which one of the two is *really* the most important? They cannot both be in center stage: if one is the star, the other will be the sidekick. If one is placed in the center, the other will be marginalized and find itself in the periphery, and, ultimately, will be merely tolerated. To say we need both subject-centered and student-centered education sounds friendly and kind. In actuality, by simply combining them we are likely to end up exalting the one and demeaning the other. I suggest that you consider a different framework within which to place subjects and students.

What kind of framework? Well, for starters, we will have to avoid reductionisms. We cannot look at "subject-centeredness" and "student-centeredness" as two independent, complete-in-themselves, competing entities. Maybe we can avoid the reductionism if we rephrase the original question. Rather than asking, "Should our school be subject-centered or student-centered?" we could pose the question this way: "How do subject matter and student learning meet the central purpose of our school?"

I must stop now. There are two students at the door who need to see me.

Dad

Subject: Framework
From: Lisa
To: Dad
Date: Mon, 23 Oct 15:44:20 -0700 (PDT)

Hi Dad,

I just got your letter. I think much of what you suggested is fine. I understand the dangers of reductionism and unrealistic expectations when choosing one approach over the other. But I really can't imagine what kind of new framework there might be. I don't see how rephrasing the question as "How do subject matter and student learning meet the central purpose of the school?" solves the problems you described. How does putting it this way provide a different framework? Doesn't this question still leave us stuck? Can't I just answer the question by saying that the central purpose of our school is to teach our students subject matter? That would bring us right back into subject-centeredness, wouldn't it? Or I could respond: Our school provides a setting in which the children can naturally develop their God-given potential. Now we end up in progressivism again (Christianized a bit by adding "God-given"). No Dad, you are going to have to do better. Please elaborate. I'll wait for your response.

Love, Lisa

Subject: Re: Framework
From: Dad
To: Lisa
Date: Mon, 23 Oct 17:48:22 -0500 (CDT)

Dear Lisa,

Let me try to clarify what I had in mind. The debates about students versus subjects—as well as all the other polarities I mentioned earlier—are indeed dependent on our view of the purpose of education. So if you are to address the issue meaningfully in your committee, you need to return to the larger biblical framework that begins with the affirmation that schools are institutions for teaching and learning. Schools cannot do their task without subject matter and students.

Most important, schools are for equipping students to function as knowledgeable and competent disciples of the Lord. Putting it this way no longer pits subject matter over against the students. Subject matter and skills are placed as indispensable ingredients in a larger schooling process.

So what sort of framework might you depict in your report? I suggest you picture a kind of spiraling, interactive process. Schooling begins with students. Let's make sure, by the way, that we do not think of students as merely minds in bodies or, even worse, as empty containers. Rather, they are gifted, experienced, contributing creatures of God. In schools they are introduced to and interact with subject matter in order to learn the competencies required for responsible discipleship. Let's also be sure that we work with a very broad concept of subject matter. Too often we think of subject matter as narrow, separate fields of study, or as the "basics." Instead, let's reaffirm that subject matter is as wide as God's world. Subject matter should be seen as opportunities to explore God's creation rather than merely content to be mastered.

Students interact not only with a broad range of subject matter, but also with the teacher as a person, the classroom environment, peers, and everything else that makes a school a school. None of these factors have any meaning without all the others. Together they form a seamless, educational whole. Each one of them is an aspect of a process that spirals from beginning acquaintance to deepening insight.

Once reductionism sets in, however, we begin to think thoughts such as these: "The subject matter is most important. I must cover the material. I have no time to consider the students as unique persons with unique needs," or "The student is obviously the important thing—subject matter is insignificant; it makes little difference what content we teach the kids." When we think such thoughts, Lisa, we are in trouble. We are then on the verge of getting caught in a treadmill of polarizations and pendulum swings.

What does the spiraling interactive framework suggest in practice? Well, for one thing, teachers need to think carefully about the instructional strategies they use and the classroom environment they construct. A teacher cannot simply toss subject matter at the students without considering their different gifts, needs, and learning styles. In practice, a unit will probably be taught differently each year because the students are different each year. The subject matter itself may need continual adjustment in order to insure optimum learning.

I have only sketched a general context for you, Lisa. You and your committee may wish to consider these suggestions, elaborate on them, and make them clear to the constituency.

Send me a copy of your report, okay?

As always, Dad

6

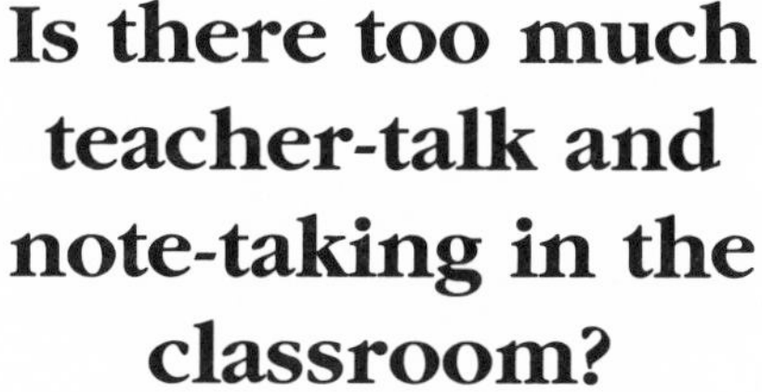

Is there too much teacher-talk and note-taking in the classroom?

Oct. 22

Hi Dad,

Time for a snail-mail letter. It's Sunday evening. So far the semester has gone okay, I think. As time goes on, I do seem to be busier and busier. Why are we always so busy? Well, maybe I should have said "No" to the invitation to chair the special study committee.

Anyway, after a few months it gets harder and harder to plan good, creative units. It's so much easier just to tell the kids what they should know, have them write down some notes, and give a test or two.

That routine reminds me of an interesting debate I overheard in the staff lounge. I think a journal article on the table fueled the argument. The article, probably written from a constructivist point of view, suggested that teachers should, as much as possible, eliminate direct instruction from their classrooms, and substitute hands-on "active learning."

The fourth-grade teacher, Jennifer, obviously endorsed this approach, but Ken, a middle school teacher, was not so sure. "Why should I change?" he asked. "Direct instruction is an efficient and effective way of teaching. A well-crafted lecture, for example, can convey all the important information kids need to know in a minimum amount of time. When you lecture, you can be sure that all the students will have the basic facts. And it is easy to manage the class when you teach in this way: you keep the kids on task by having them listen to you and take notes. Besides," he argued, "all this fancy stuff about group work and cooperative learning is still untested. It still looks to me like an exercise in pooling ignorance!"

Well, to make a long story short, Jennifer saw the issue quite differently. She cited figures taken from other journal articles that suggest students forget more than 50% of their notes within a month after they write them down! Besides, she thinks that having the kids write notes is altogether too dull a way to teach!

I think, Dad, that here's another sample of what you call polarizations. It's either one thing or another. Direct teaching or active learning. What a ridiculous way of putting it! I think even the most hardened constructivist has to make use of direct instruction. Just to get kids to do things—to get them ready for active learning, for example—requires explanations of some kind. The kids will need directions and instructions—plenty of teacher talk—to which students will have to respond. Eliminating direct instruction from a classroom is a silly idea.

I think, too, Dad, that lecturing and note-taking can be quite interactive, especially if the teacher stops frequently and asks questions, or asks the kids to summarize or explain or raise issues. She could even ask her kids to stick their heads together and come up with suggestions from their experience or assigned readings. It seems to me I've heard you talk about this approach as "participatory lecturing" or some such thing.

You know what? It suddenly occurred to me that when we polarize in this way, we actually caricature the two poles as well. Educational debates almost always end up with caricatured pictures. They distort the opposing view in order to win the argument. I thought you'd be interested in hearing about this. I've heard you talk about polarizations and fads, but not about caricaturing. Maybe I can claim that idea as an original. Just call me Professor Lisa! :)

Well, Dad, I should turn in. I am actually planning to have my kids take quite a few notes tomorrow!

Love,

Lisa

Wednesday, October 25

Dear Lisa,

Thanks for your interesting letter. Your point about caricatures is very well made. It reminds me of how conservatives and liberals caricature the opposing side. But you are right: in an educational debate the opposing positions tend to be painted in unrealistic terms, and probably in reductionistic terms as well, don't you think? For example, when direct teaching is caricatured as the enemy of active learning, something valuable in direct instruction has been suppressed or eliminated altogether. Direct instruction has been made to appear less than what it really is.

At the same time, reductionisms frequently distort some basic truth. The teacher-talk and note-taking approach, for example, like any other teaching strategy, becomes a problem when it is overused. Much of the popular criticism of lecturing, as expressed by constructivists and progressivists, is criticism of *excessive use* of lectures and teacher-talk. Too much of it changes students into passive receptacles and leaves them uninvolved in their learning, and in the long run, bored and turned off.

I think there is reason for concern on this point. Not so long ago I observed a fourth-grade teacher actually lecture for nearly forty minutes, while the children copied down notes, quietly and without any opportunity to ask questions or respond. It may well be that here was a "top-down pedagogy" at work: this fourth-grade teacher imitated middle school teachers who imitate high school teachers who imitate their lecturing college professors. I suspect that most educators would frown on this fourth-grade teacher. And for good reasons. Let me identify three consequences of an overdose of teacher-talk that worry me.

The first is that such a teaching style goes hand-in-hand with whole-class instruction and, consequently, tends to ignore different learning styles. As you know from your own experience, some children do fine listening to the teacher and learning a set of notes. But others need much more variety, and have to get involved in the lessons in a much more concrete, hands-on, active way. This is true not only for first and second graders, but for *all* elementary *and* secondary students.

Secondly, too much teacher-talk allows the spirit of individualism to flourish in a classroom. When students are listening to the teacher all the time, they have very little opportunity to interact with each other and to work on their task of helping build a community in the classroom. Their concern will be limited to making sure that they, as individuals, get the information straight and know how to regurgitate it to the teacher. There will be no responsibility for each other's learning. So a really Christian, collaborative classroom, a classroom in which the Body of Christ can come to expression, will be difficult to develop.

My third worry concerns the very real problem of passivity. Let's face it, when the teacher does all the talking and the children all the listening, a one-way street situation inevitably develops. It's like listening to someone go on and on in a telephone call without being able to get a word in edgewise. The teacher transmits knowledge and the students *receive* knowledge. They become "receptacles"—some teachers think "empty-headed receptacles"—and such receptivity snuggles up to passivity. Now why is this a problem? Two reasons: first, because such passivity breeds, I believe, selfishness. The students learn to expect things—including knowledge—to be dished up on a silver platter, ready for consumption, without much expenditure of effort and energy. Taking notes and memorizing materials is actually a lazy learner's way. I realize I'm in danger of caricaturing here, but you know what I mean. I am talking about the sort of teaching that emphasizes the mastery of much factual content to the virtual exclusion of critical reflection or deep understanding.

A second, more alarming problem with student passivity is that it reflects an attitude quite incompatible with the ultimate goal of Christian teaching: knowledgeable and competent discipleship. To be a disciple of the Lord in our complicated world requires a lot of knowledge and a lot of competence. Especially required is an active, willing-to-reach-out disposition. A disciple of Jesus does not sit around waiting for things to happen. On the contrary, a disciple actively and aggressively looks for ways to exercise servanthood.

Sometimes it is argued that teacher-talk/student-listening is the Christian way of teaching. Doesn't Deuteronomy tell us to "imprint" the truth on the minds of our impressionable youngsters? But it is interesting to note that Jesus himself often used parables to teach. He could have sat his disciples down and said to them, "Okay, you guys, get out pencil and paper and take down the following notes!" But he didn't. More often than not he told stories with hidden meanings. He put the disciples to work. They had to think. They had to come up—actively—with the real meaning of the parables. Jesus did not present his lessons on a silver platter. He actively involved his students in their learning. And, of course, he *really* got them involved when he sent them out two by two. Talk about hands-on learning!

Let me stop here, Lisa, and acknowledge that you are right on target when you point to the foolishness of polarizing direct instruction and active learning, as if direct instruction does not involve student activity and as if active learning is free from teacher talk. It is only when we rely too much on one or another strategy that we run into trouble. Only when most of the conversation in the classroom consists of the teacher talking do we need to rethink our teaching styles.

The conclusion of the matter is this: Whatever teaching methods we use and whatever we call them—direct instruction, active learning, or what not—we must use them appropriately. How? Well, we begin with the assumption that our classroom should be a community breathing a safe, secure, Christian atmosphere. In such a classroom we may use a variety of strategies, ranging from direct teaching to cooperative learning, creative dramatics, and storytelling. Most of us teachers, I fear, do tend to talk too much in our classrooms, and thereby reduce opportunities for the students to participate in and act on their learning, and restrict possibilities for constructing community in the classroom. Using a tape recorder in our classrooms to check ourselves is often a revealing tool.

See once what Jennifer and Ken say about these ruminations. If you can persuade them to back off from their either/or positions, you will have done them a service!

Dad

7

Should I get rid of worksheets?

Saturday, October 28

Dear Lisa,

In response to your telephone call earlier today, I decided to sit down and write yet another letter to you. I hope you don't get the feeling that I am telling you what to do. I appreciate it when you remind me that although I am your father, you are a professional teacher and no longer a little child who needs to be given instructions. Nevertheless, your most recent concern merits a response. As I heard it, you suddenly feel inadequate after your conversation with Sheila, the other fifth-grade teacher in the school. You worry that Sheila is much more successful at teaching her students the basic skills than you are. You *know* that Sheila uses more worksheets than you do—in fact, she is at the photocopying machine every time you need to use it—so probably her students get loads more practice learning skills than yours do, you think.

Now before you decide to compete with Sheila and start cranking out the paper, let's take stock for just a minute. You know and I know that you are a good teacher. If there is a reason to lose confidence, it had better be something other than Sheila's worksheet mania.

Let's talk about this worksheet business for a bit, shall we? Sometimes I see teachers who appear to be genuine "worksheetaholics": they think teaching without worksheets is unthinkable. The standardized test craze fuels their belief. These teachers assume a direct correlation between high test scores and the number of worksheets. This assumption prompts the worksheetaholics to put the photocopying machine into overdrive.

It takes no deep thinker to see why teachers gravitate to worksheets like paper clips to a magnet. Let's face it: worksheets make teaching look mighty easy, especially if you fall heir to the teacher's manual with pre-fabricated worksheets. But even if you construct them yourself, worksheets are handy tools to have around. They are a great management device: nothing looks so well-managed as a roomful of children diligently and quietly doing their worksheets. That scene scores big with some visiting school board members!

There are other advantages as well. While the students are doing their worksheets, you will have time to sit at your desk to catch up on your grading. You can take a welcome break from *active* teaching. And for ease of grading, worksheets are the thing: an aide can score them, if need be. Or you can use worksheet time to assist students who need special help.

Worksheets also function nicely as assessment instruments. By looking at worksheets you can right away see which students are falling behind. If most of them do well on worksheets, you will have reasons to crow, like Sheila; you will sense measurable progress and be completely convinced that your youngsters have really learned. And—let's not forget it—you can send graded worksheets home with the children. In your mind you can see the satisfied parents nod with approval as they see all that work accomplished; no doubt they will be sure to remind the principal of your teaching effectiveness!

So you see, Lisa, that it makes good sense for a teacher to go heavy on the worksheets. Now before we conclude that hey! worksheets are *the* ticket to a successful teaching career, let's ask an important question: Is the emphasis on worksheets really in the best interest of *Christian* teaching? Should I encourage you to use as many worksheets as Sheila does? Will it make you a more effective *Christian* teacher?

Recently I spent some time in a classroom with one of those worksheetaholic teachers. It was a language arts class. The students had to circle nouns and adjectives on a worksheet. They were sitting in their desks, and it looked as if a great deal of learning was going on. The teacher looked pleased. Once in a while she would get up to respond to a raised hand.

The more I watched, however, the more I noticed some disturbing items. Item number one: all the students were working individually in their neat rows. I wondered, if the teacher insists on using worksheets, why not structure the activity so that the children will learn how to work together and help each other (as I see many other Christian teachers do)? I also noticed that some students finished their worksheets in a flash. Obviously smart kids, I said to myself. The teacher had announced that those who finished early could take the extra time to read their books or to work on other assignments. I asked myself: How come these youngsters who finished their language arts worksheets early are not given opportunity to stretch their linguistic skills further? Could it be that the worksheet imposes a ceiling on their achievement? Finish your worksheet and nothing more needs to be learned?

At the same time, I observed other students struggling with the worksheet. Just walking around and looking at their efforts, I could easily see that obviously some of these children had no clue as to what nouns and adjectives were, and were simply guessing. Surprisingly, they often guessed right! They were learning, not nouns and adjectives, but patterns and procedures that make it *appear* that they understood. I have observed this phenomenon in math classes as well. They know *what* to do, but have no idea why. At one point I saw a student ask another for help. A third student, obviously one who knew what he was doing, turned around and looked in a way that said it all: you dummy!

Now wait a minute, someone will object: What I am describing is not the fault of worksheets as much as the teacher's problem. She should have used some group work, given additional worksheets to the top students, and reprimanded the kid who calls others dummies!

True, worksheets are not inherently evil. But unless teachers are careful, heavy use of worksheets can foster individualism, discourage gifted students, and create opportunities for some to look at others with disdain. Now in case you think I am just being ornery, let me mention some other classroom headaches that reliance on worksheets invite.

A really big problem is that many worksheets focus on single, isolated skills. Ten sets of worksheets often require practice in ten different skills. But often the children have no idea how the skills are related to each other or to life as a whole: a transfer problem, in other words. The skills learned on worksheets often are not applied to other situations. And what about learning styles, individual gifts, and individual needs? Worksheets assume that all students are at the same level, and they are prejudiced in favor of those who are linguistically and visually talented. But what about the children who demonstrate learning most clearly through hands-on, auditory, or dramatic activities? They are left behind in the dust, I fear.

I am especially concerned about the passivity that worksheets promote. Stacks of worksheets call for mere identification and recognition (like circling nouns and adjectives). In science classes, many worksheets and exercises require only a meek following of procedures in order to come to predicted and predetermined results: do this and this and this, then such and such should happen. Such worksheets stifle creativity and curiosity, and prevent students from experiencing the thrill of discovery. Ultimately such worksheets shut down learning and keep our children from developing skills for active discipleship.

So should we throw out worksheets altogether? Or do they display some redeeming features? Lisa, I suggest that whenever you feel the urge or temptation to use worksheets, ask yourself some penetrating questions. Maybe the following checklist of questions will help. Even before you use this checklist, decide to use worksheets sparingly. Decide firmly that you will not be a slave to the worksheet. Decide right now that in your teaching you will use worksheets only in a *supplementary* fashion, not as the kingpin of your teaching practice. If you plan to use worksheets in math, for example, be sure you have taken the children through an extensive series of manipulatives first, and then continue to use the manipulatives to make the worksheet numbers real. Now let's look at the checklist of questions:

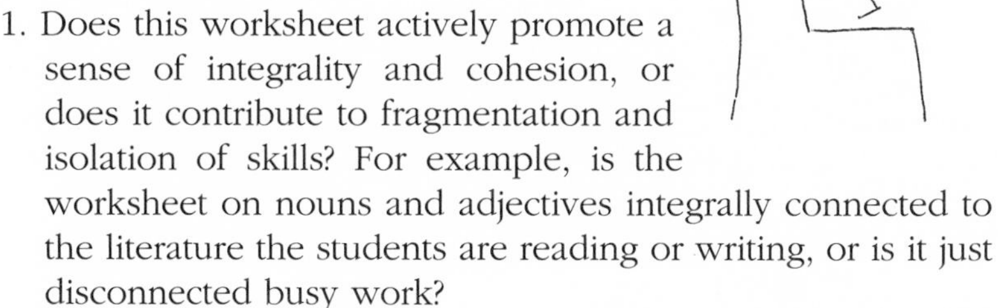

1. Does this worksheet actively promote a sense of integrality and cohesion, or does it contribute to fragmentation and isolation of skills? For example, is the worksheet on nouns and adjectives integrally connected to the literature the students are reading or writing, or is it just disconnected busy work?

2. How will this worksheet activity address individual learning styles, student gifts, or student needs? Will it cap achievement or encourage further exploration? Will this worksheet address only one dominant learning style and so by-pass many of your students?

3. Will the worksheet contribute to the development of active, critical thinking skills, promote curiosity and creativity, and lead to what we have called the thrill of discovery? Or is it merely routine drudgery?

4. Finally, will the students *enjoy* the worksheet activity? Will they see it as significant and relevant to their learning and their lives, or will it be another groan-evoking assignment?

The bottom-line question is: Can you see, in broad strokes, that the worksheets will contribute to the development of discipleship? Will they really help equip your students for works of service?

Now think back to your conversation with Sheila. Then dump your worries about being a second-rate teacher. Just smile sweetly when she gets to the photocopy machine before you do!

Dad

8

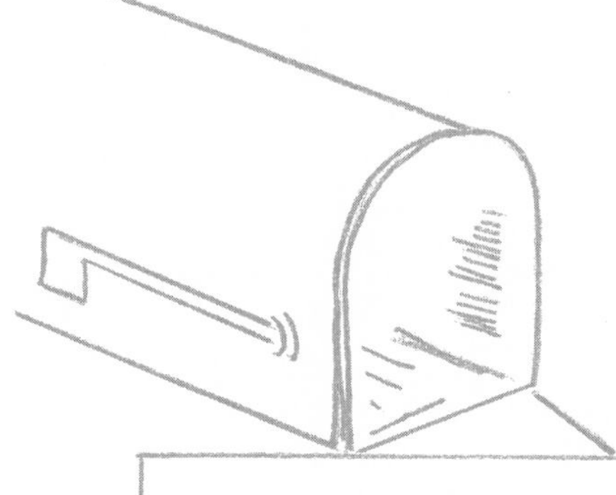

Is there a Christian way to ask questions in the classroom?

Subject: Questions
From: Lisa
To: Dad
Date: Tue, 31 Oct 16:00:24 -0800 (PST)

Hi Dad,

I taught a lesson this afternoon that obviously was tailor-made for asking questions. But guess what: I can already begin to see some of my fifth-graders lose their spontaneous curiosity—seems to be part of schooling. Ask a question in the first grade, and pow! the classroom explodes into a throng of waving hands and "me me me's." But by the sixth and seventh grades, I'm told, a sort of stony inertia begins to set in. What do you think, Dad? Could it be that what we teach (and ask questions about) is less and less relevant to the lives of the kids as they move through the grade levels? Could it be that the structure of our schools increasingly encourages passive compliance and docility rather than excitement about learning?

My students' blank response started my thinking about the art of asking questions. Do you think that there is a distinctively Christian approach to questioning techniques in the classroom? Or are questions simply questions, no matter who asks them? We're supposed to do everything to the glory of God. Well, how can I honor God in the way I ask the kids questions?

Love, Lisa

Subject: Re: Questions
From: Dad
To: Lisa
Date: Tue, 31 Oct 18:30:41 -0600 (CST)

Dear Lisa,

Is there a way to ask questions Christianly? You know the answer, of course. It's yes. There *has* to be. Look at it this way: Questioning students in the classroom is part of teaching, right? And there is a difference between simply teaching—you know, simply following the manual, for example—and teaching Christianly, right? If Christ is Lord of all, He is Lord over our teaching *and* questioning. Let's take a closer look.

You realize that there are all sorts of good reasons for asking students questions in class. Questions serve as good discussion starters, give you a handle on how well the students are grasping what you are trying to teach them, and encourage reflection and communication. By not repeating student responses you teach the children to listen to each other. And when you allow plenty of "wait time," you promote good thinking.

Now it is also important that you try to get *everyone* to respond. You know how it is: some children are always ready to answer a question, while others resemble mummies. Don't hesitate to address the quieter students. Use various methods to make sure every student gets a turn. You could, for example, put the names of your students in a box and pull one out every time you ask a question. Just for fun, you might give Tim or Stephanie a class list. One of them could keep track for a day of who responds to questions. You may be surprised at what you will discover!

Recall, too, the distinction between different types of questions. Look at these examples: (1) When was Julius Caesar assassinated? (2) How many uses for a rotten tomato can you think of? The first question has only one right answer. The second one has multiple answers, none more correct than any of the others. It is the difference between convergent and divergent questions, remember? Studies show that 80% of all the questions teachers pose in the classroom are simple, factual, convergent, fill-in-the-blank type questions. Such questions promote little more than memorization and recall. Check to see what kinds of questions you ask your youngsters. Be sure to include plenty of divergent questions. Encourage your students to think and evaluate.

All of this is basic review, of course. Now let me get to the issue at stake. How can we think Christianly about our classroom questioning strategies? Now suppose you're a positivist of the deepest dye, a teacher who believes that good learning consists of the accumulation of swarms of facts. The educated person is the quiz show whiz-kid. What sorts of questions is such a teacher likely to pose? Why, only-one-right-answer *convergent* questions, of course. The questions will have a narrow focus. Their scope is limited. If, on the other hand, you were a strict progressivist, a teacher who believes that the primary purpose of education is to turn our students into effective problem-solvers, you would avoid convergent questions, wouldn't you? You would go for the divergent sort, that is, your questions would prompt thinking and analysis instead of ability to recall. So again, but in a different way, the progressivist's scope of questioning is limited.

You see, your educational philosophy has everything to do with classroom questioning. Not only does the scope of your questions reflect your basic philosophy, your questions also point towards a direction: they always have a purpose, they always take the students somewhere. The crucial question is: Where do your questions lead your students? What is the direction?

For you and me the answer is pretty clear: We want our students to walk in the ways of the Lord. This means that you cannot be satisfied with always asking simple, factual questions, important and appropriate though they may be at times. Your questions have to go deeper, beyond facts and figuring; they must reach into the lives of your children. Ultimately your questions must lead to meaningful reflection about values, priorities, feelings, and commitments: What do your students feel and believe about the subject matter you are teaching them? How do they see the subject matter affecting their lives? Of course, you cannot ask questions like these in every lesson. But plan to ask them somewhere, at regular intervals, in your unit.

Let me know if these musings make sense to you, okay?

As ever, Dad

Subject: More questions
From: Lisa
To: Dad
Date: Tue, 31 Oct 17:14:55 -0800 (PST)

Hi Dad,

Yes, what you've said makes perfect sense. But aren't you forgetting something? I mean, sure, this business about types and scope of questions and all that *is* important. But shouldn't we also be concerned about *how* we ask questions? For example, I think we should model a gentle, sensitive way of questioning. I have no tolerance for put-downs and sarcasm. Don't you agree?

Love, Lisa

Subject: Re: More questions
From: Dad
To: Lisa
Date: Tue, 31 Oct 19:24:22 -0600 (CST)

Dear Lisa,

Yes, I agree completely. And let me offer some other examples of how we might conduct our classroom questioning in a Christian way. I think it's important, Lisa, that we really listen to our students' responses. We should look for what they *intend* to say, rather than merely judging *what* they say. We should train ourselves to listen, so that we won't make hasty judgments. Too quickly we judge a response to be wrong or irrelevant, when in fact the student is well on the way to expressing profound understanding. Or we simply misunderstand a response. So be sure to listen, and to encourage students to repeat a response in different words or ask another student for an interpretation. Before you dismiss a response, reformulate your initial question. Remember, gentleness and patience are fruits of the Spirit that have a direct bearing on how you deal with student responses.

Another point. To think Christianly about questioning requires that we consider not only the why and how, but also the place *where* we ask questions. Questions are never posed in a vacuum; they always assume a context—the context of individual lessons, to be sure, but in the larger sense, the context of the classroom. One cannot ask questions Christianly, if, for example, the classroom in which they are asked is thick with fear and suspicion. In such classrooms, children will be afraid of asking and responding to questions. They will fear making mistakes or appearing stupid. So we need a Christian, collaborative classroom where we encourage and support each other, where all questions are welcome, and where there is no place for fear of being wrong or being put down.

For that reason, Lisa, avoid always directing your questions to individual students. If, as a general rule, you solicit individual responses only, you encourage the children to compete for right answers. You create tension in your classroom. When both Tim and Stephanie raise their hand in response to a question, both confident they know the answer, Tim may secretly hope that, if she gets recognized, Stephanie will give the wrong answer. Individual questioning encourages the students to vie for your attention and your approval. They learn to hope that others are wrong, for that increases the chances that they will shine. The success of one student, in other words, begins to depend on the failure of others.

To avoid this problem, frequently ask your students to stick their heads together and come up with group answers, especially in response to significant questions. And be sure to encourage the children to ask questions of each other and to respond to each other. The more you get the students to interact, the more successful you will be at establishing and maintaining a Christian, collaborative classroom.

One final bit of advice: When it comes to questioning in your classroom, be sure that from the very beginning you make your expectations clear. Discuss with the students just what kind of classroom you aim to conduct, and invite them to suggest the expected behavior. Whenever you hear a put-down or sarcasm, stop the proceedings right there and review the expectations you and your youngsters have established for yourselves.

The fact that you are asking questions about asking questions, Lisa, means that you are a reflective practitioner—a reflective, *Christian* practitioner. Many of my suggestions probably are mere review for you. However, from my own experience I know that some things about teaching we need to review and review and review some more, until the day we retire.

Keep thinking, Lisa, and keep asking good questions!

As ever, Dad

9

How important is the atmosphere in my classroom?

Subject: Classroom atmosphere
From: Lisa
To: Dad
Date: Thu, 2 Nov 16:34:16 -0800 (PST)

Hi Dad,

Today was one of my annual professional days. The school pays for a substitute so I can go off to another school to observe a fifth-grade teacher—a great opportunity to learn, let me tell you! I think every school should have such a program. It's so rare that we teachers see other teachers teach.

Anyway, the teacher I observed this morning was one of those no-nonsense, on-task persons. She believes that the best learning occurs when you maintain a strict, business-like, don't-smile-until-Christmas classroom environment. Her style reminds me of what the effective teaching movement has been endorsing for years: on-task efficiency. During the coffee break I asked her if such an approach is compatible with the idea of teaching Christianly. Yes, she thought, for, after all, we are to be stewards of our time, and we're in the classroom to get the students to learn, not to entertain them with fun and games. One can create a good learning environment, she said, by concentrating on teaching strategies and learning activities. As long as they are effective—meaning, I suppose, that the kids score high on tests—we need not be too concerned about classroom atmosphere.

What do you think about this approach, Dad? To be honest, it makes me feel very uncomfortable. It seems to me that Christian teachers should be very concerned about creating a positive, wholesome, friendly atmosphere in their classrooms. And such an atmosphere may mean lightening up on this on-task business. I don't want my classroom to be a boot camp with me as the drill sergeant. Of course, neither do I want a circus where I'm the ringmaster or perhaps even the clown!

What is your view of classroom atmosphere, Dad?

Love, Lisa

Friday, November 3

Dear Lisa,

Your e-mail reached me at a propitious time. I have been doing a bit of research on the question of classroom atmosphere for a staff development workshop next week. I'm glad you enjoyed the opportunity to get out of your own classroom and to see someone else teach. Does your principal require you to write a brief report about what you learned and how the visit might affect your own teaching? Sometimes principals even ask the teachers to share their observations at staff meetings: a good idea!

Rather than dashing off an e-mail message back to you, I decided to sit down and write a letter. I find it easier to think that way. The question of classroom environment merits careful reflection.

What might be some basic biblical principles we can turn to when we think about our classrooms? Well, one of them leaps out of the book, it seems to me: the theme of community. When you were a little baby, Lisa, your mother and I brought you into our church to be baptized. Other Christian parents dedicate their young children. Of course, you little ones have no clue what is happening. If I remember correctly, you hollered a good deal and even spit up on your special gown. But by baptizing you we declared, before the entire congregation, that you are one of God's precious children, and we promised to do everything in our power to bring you up in a way pleasing to the Lord. In other words, we inducted you, as it were, into a community of Christian brothers and sisters.

In the Old Testament I see the story of a community, God's chosen people wandering about and settling down in the midst of deadly enemies. The theme of community carries right over into the New Testament: now no longer a tradition-bound ethnic group of Hebrews, but a community which includes Gentiles and stretches to the ends of the earth. Now it is called the church, the *ecclesia,* the Christian community, the Body of Christ.

"But Dad," you will object, "not every one of my students is a Christian. So your talk about Body of Christ and this thing called *ecclesia* is not really relevant. I still have a herd of heathens to contend with!"

Let me address this likely objection. Do you suppose that you must wait with establishing a community atmosphere in your class until you know for sure that every student is fully committed? If we were to adopt the 100% commitment as a guiding principle, we would have to close the doors of every single church! For there is not a congregation in which we would not find an unbeliever or two. Augustine already recognized this reality when he wrote about the two cities, the City of God and the Worldly City, and about the intermixture of the two. Everywhere we go, whether into our classrooms or even into our hearts, we find both wheat and tares.

The question is not: Who is in my class and who is not in my class? or Do I have the right sort of students to start thinking about a classroom community? Rather, we should ask: What should my classroom look like? In sum, we must *begin* with the assumption that we *will* establish community; only *then* do we look at our students. We have to muster some boldness here. The scarcity of real community out there in the world should not prevent me, a Christian teacher, from slogging away to create community, at least in my own classroom. So I say, Lisa, let's go for it! Let's find out how far we can push this community thing before we bump into snags and roadblocks. Let's do our best to model community. Some of the students may reject it, but we'll cross that bridge when we come to it.

Now there is another biblical principle we must not overlook. It is this: we humans were created to love and serve God and one another. Our classrooms ought to be places where the children are not only *told* to be loving and kind, but also get plenty of opportunity to *practice* love and kindness. Often we tell the students how to behave. We preach. But if the preaching is not translated into specific practice, it won't have much effect. I'm reminded of the chapel sessions I sometimes observe in Christian schools. The local minister comes in and preaches a slam-bang sermon on the fruit of the Spirit. Be kind and gentle and what not. But such preaching goes in and out of both ears, when, in the hallways and classes that follow, conversations are peppered with bad language. So you see, Lisa, we must design classroom situations and exercises which foster a range of discipleship and servanthood skills. In fact, our lesson plans and goal statements should say much about such skills.

Think of it this way: When you teach fractions, do you just *tell* the children about such things? Well, yes, you do; but you also have them practice *doing* fractions. It is only through practice that they begin to understand and apply the mathematical concepts you teach them. So it is with love and service. Talking about them is one thing; practicing them is another.

Love God above all and your neighbor as yourself. This talk about love is no religious babble! We are dealing with rock-bottom fundamentals here. Loving service lies at the heart of the Christian life. It lies at the center of all human life—*and* of life in the classroom. Without it, all the academic stuff we teach doesn't amount to a single slice of banana cream pie. As Paul puts it in a famous chapter I like to quote: if I have all the knowledge in the world but have not love, I am nothing.

In short, when we reflect on the sort of classroom atmosphere we want to forge, let's think of the importance of a loving, serving community. True, some parents will be critical and demand an ambitious, self-seeking, no-nonsense atmosphere. To them talk about love and service is a covey of warm fuzzies.

Please, Lisa, do not permit yourself to be cornered by such demands. If you cave in, you may end up with a classroom where students are out for themselves and where you will have to function like a heartless taskmaster. In such a classroom trust will be replaced by suspicion, love by self-centeredness, and service by unhealthy competition. You cannot teach Christianly in such a classroom.

You saw such a classroom on your professional visit day—at least, a classroom on the way to becoming a hard, cold place. I sometimes see more "advanced" versions. You can almost feel and touch the fear in such classrooms: fear of the teacher, fear of each other, fear of the principal, and fear of failure. Such classrooms flatly contradict what we know from Scripture: Love casts out fear. On numerous occasions Jesus admonishes his followers: Fear not! Don't be afraid. If Jesus were to walk into your classroom, would he have to say, "Don't be afraid!" to you and your students?

"Well," you say, "all of this is well and good and I agree with all these lofty principles, but how am I going to put them into practice? You should see the kids I have to teach, and the sort of families they come from! Even *you* would be appalled!"

Okay, I did not say that creating a Christian classroom is an easy task. But it's not an impossible task. Decide firmly, Lisa, that you will not succumb to pragmatistic "Can it be done?" worries. Instead, redouble your efforts to construct a classroom environment pleasing to the Lord.

Naturally I would appreciate hearing about your successes, and about the problems as well, of course. So stay in touch.

Dad

Subject: Atmosphere
From: Lisa
To: Dad
Date: Tue, 7 Nov 15:35:59 -0800 (PST)

Hi Dad,

Thanks for your encouragement. I do really want to build the sort of classroom atmosphere you describe. But it all sounds a bit theoretical and unreal to me. Just yesterday, for example, there was this spat between Keith and Jeffrey. I had trouble settling them down. You talked about bad language. Well, you should hear *these* kids! A loving, caring classroom atmosphere seems so far removed from the real thing.

If you have some time, I'd like to hear some specifics.

Love, Lisa

Tuesday evening, November 7

Dear Lisa,

Yes, there is of course much more to say. Let me share some points I plan to make in my workshop. Recent literature suggests that the way we organize our classroom has much to do with the atmosphere we bring about. In most classrooms, the structure is one of individualism. In such a classroom each individual child is responsible to the teacher alone for his or her learning. In such a classroom the learning of one student is not related to that of any of the others. When Jeffrey fails, even after numerous

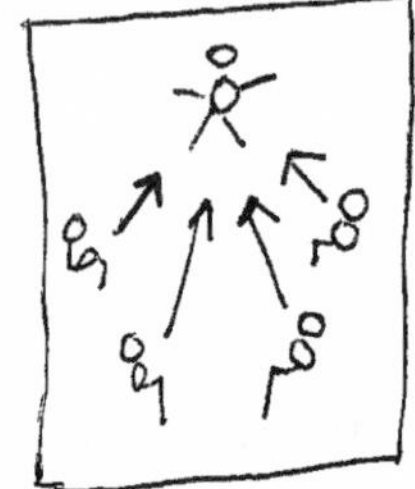

tries, well, that is of no concern to Tim. And Tim's success, in turn, means nothing to Jeffrey.

You recognize at once, I'm sure, the fundamental flaw in such a classroom. The biblical meaning of community demands that if one part of the body hurts, the whole body hurts. And when one person rejoices, we all celebrate. I Corinthians 12:26 provides a clear guideline here. Jeffrey's difficulties should be painful to the entire class, including Tim. And the whole class should be eager to crow about Tim's good work.

Don't overlook the fact that individualism has its roots in ancient pagan Greek philosophy. The Sophists, Cynics, and Stoics, for example, preached a gospel of independency and self-sufficiency. During the Middle Ages individualism went underground for a while. But later, at the time of the Renaissance, it reemerged with a frenzy, this time adorned with notions of individualistic/autonomous/we-are-a-law-unto-ourselves trappings. This sort of pagan, secular, God-eliminating individualism has never left us. It has become integral to our culture. Sadly, we have begun to regard it as a normal ingredient of Western society.

Note that I am speaking of individualism—a term that ends in an "ism." Whenever we encounter an -ism, a red flag should wave vigorously in our consciousness. An -ism always suggests a distortion and an exaggeration of something true and beautiful. Like other -isms, individualism has it partly right. Of course we are unique individuals. But we are always individuals within the bonds of relationships and community. Individualism overlooks these bonds entirely.

Check yourself, Lisa. Is your classroom indeed an individualistic sort of situation? Do you ask your students to interact with each other only periodically, so that genuine community will forever elude you? Are your students encouraged, perhaps unintentionally or inadvertently, to seek their own welfare at the expense of others? Hard questions to answer, aren't they?

Sometimes individualistically-structured classrooms become competitive classrooms. In such a classroom the learning of one student does affect that of the others, but negatively. In such a classroom the success of one requires the failure of another. Grading on the curve is the crassest example I can think of. Such practice is incompatible with teaching Christianly, in my opinion.

Sometimes the competitive nature of a classroom may not be immediately evident. It can hide beneath layers of feelings. For example, it is present whenever one student begrudges the success of another. It may be deep-seated, as in Marci's silent, secret hope that Stephanie will respond wrongly to the teacher's question. It may momentarily become visible when you see a smirk of disdain on Shelley's face when she discovers that Jeffrey got a much lower grade than she did on an essay. It can be present even in the simple question-and-answer lesson, in which students vie with each other for the teacher's attention and approval.

Oh, the challenge of being a truly Christian teacher! How impossible it seems to avoid the pitfalls of individualism and competition. Add to this the large classes, the busy schedule, the grading and marking and all the bureaucratic stuff we teachers are saddled with, and you can see why it is so easy to give in to the temptation to forget about this classroom atmosphere stuff and just teach.

Don't! Don't cave in, Lisa. Keep struggling for what ought to be. Keep the faith and keep the vision, even though at times discouragement and depression make it difficult for you to go on. Keep reminding yourself that classroom atmosphere is important. Keep telling yourself that you will not stand for an individualistic or competitive classroom.

I recognize that I am preaching now. Forgive me. Yet, the stuff we're discussing is critically important to teaching Christianly. I do so much want you to reaffirm your desire to fight the paganisms inherent in individualistic and competitive classrooms.

So am I saying that teachers should organize a lot of group work? Well, there's group work and then there's "simply group work." "Simply group work" is a well-meant effort to overcome the evils of competitive individualism. It is an attempt to get the children to interact and to work together. In fact, it is often confused with cooperative learning. You see children sitting in groups around tables, ostensibly working diligently and effectively together. But a closer look discloses a different picture. In actuality there are usually one or two students in each group who do all the work while the others simply ride coattails. Careful inspection reveals quite a number of such free-loading hitchhikers. And what looked like collaboration turns out to be simply another form of individualism and competition. "Simply group work" situations do not establish the atmosphere we want.

So what *do* I want? I suggest you strive to fashion a collaborative classroom. In such a classroom the theme of community is up front. It's a classroom in which the children are given plenty of opportunity to practice servanthood skills. It is a place where the learning of one affects the learning of another, not in a negative but in a positive way, where the students take responsibility not only for each other's learning but for each other's lives. It is a classroom without fear.

Recently I observed a fourth-grade classroom well on the way to realizing such an atmosphere. The teacher—a firm but loving and caring woman—spent much time gathering the children around her to rehearse the basic principles of community. She had them practice mutual concern. The children role-played conflict and brainstormed solutions. They planned ways of helping each other. In many ways this classroom resembled a happy family.

Can you turn your classroom into such an idyllic picture? Maybe not completely—just as we cannot fully eradicate the presence of the devil and his hosts. There is the lingering reality of sin. But we can work towards such a goal, prayerfully, together with the Spirit of God. How do we start?

Well, that sounds like an insulting question. You are a fine Christian teacher, Lisa, and that means that already you are well on the way. Nevertheless, I do have some suggestions you may wish to consider. But I shall leave them for another time.

Dad

10

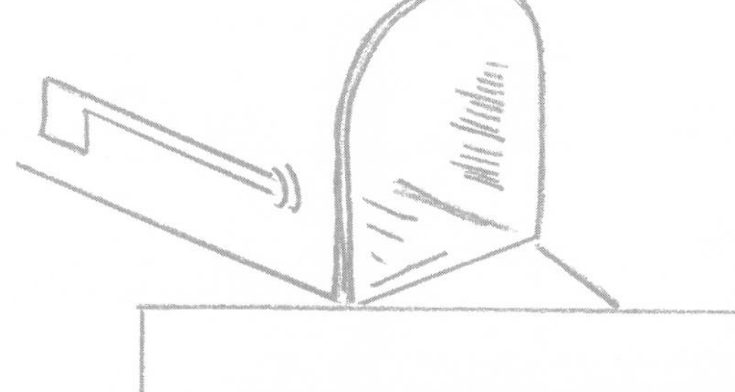

How well should I get to know my students?

Subject: Difficult kids
From: Lisa
To: Dad
Date: Mon, 13 Nov 08:03:35 -0800 (PST)

Hi Dad,

I'm running into real problems trying to work out a collaborative classroom. If only I did not have certain kids in my class. Take Keith, for example. He's causing me a lot of trouble. Sorry to sound mean, but, frankly, he is a pain! I don't understand him. No matter what I do, he disrupts the class and wrecks my lesson plans. Last week he pulled the piano over on himself! To be honest, Dad, I do think sometimes that the talk about love and peace in your previous letter is just that, nothing but talk. It's not the real world. The real world contains Keith and other unruly kids like him. Sorry to be so blunt and so negative!

Love, Lisa

Subject: Re: Difficult kids
From: Dad
To: Lisa
Date: Mon, 13 Nov 12:06:43 -0600 (CST)

Dear Lisa,

Well, what can I say? Tell you that Keith is a figment of your overtaxed imagination? Advise you to show even more love and attention than you have already given him? Pick up some assertive discipline methods and tell Keith either to shape up or ship out? I think none of this advice would do much good.

Nevertheless, I dare to raise—somewhat timidly, to be sure—a modest question: How well do you really *know* Keith? To what extent do you know what makes him tick? I wonder if not really knowing who he is might be part of the problem.

Dad

Subject: Re: Difficult kids
From: Lisa
To: Dad
Date: Mon, 13 Nov 12:11:43 -0800 (PST)

Hi Dad,

Do I know Keith? Yes, absolutely! I have the opinions of the previous teachers, cumulative files, and a battery of psychological tests. I know loads about this kid. What information would you like to have?

Frustrated, Lisa

Monday, November 13

Dear Lisa,

Okay, I hear you loud and clear. Rather than zipping off another e-mail, I've decided to sit down and write a letter. Now, at the risk of upsetting you, let me tell you something you may not like. From what you say, it seems clear to me that you have begun to *dislike* Keith. Now I realize that it is tough to like everybody. Nevertheless, I suspect your dislike for Keith is slowly but surely changing to lovelessness. And when lovelessness sets in, you no longer really *want* to know youngsters like Keith. Be honest now: If you had your druthers, would you not just as soon see Keith transferred out of your classroom rather than avail yourself of further opportunity to learn to get to know and love him? You said as much in your earlier e-mail message.

The point is this: our ability to love a person, or even just to like a person, is closely related to how well we really know the person. The motto of the Amsterdam zoo, Artis, is "*Onbekend maakt onbemind*" which translates to something like "Unknown means unloved." The less we know about frogs, toads, and snakes, the more likely we are to dislike them. The Amsterdam zoo aims to help folks love the animals with which they are not yet acquainted.

I do not want to turn you off, Lisa, by arguing that your problems with Keith stem from ignorance. I do not know enough about the situation to make such a judgment. But I do claim that teachers set themselves up for disappointment, and indeed, make establishing a collaborative classroom atmosphere impossible simply because they do not make enough effort to really get to know their students.

I would not be surprised if what I am saying irritates you. I can almost hear you stomp your foot, the way you did when you were a little girl. "Look here," you will protest, "how can you expect me to really get to know my students when I have 27 of them in my class, each one of them unique and even more complicated than the other? And what about the hapless high school teachers, some of whom see more than 150 students file through their classrooms every single school day?"

All right, I concede. Given our current school structures and student-teacher ratios, it's extremely tough. But that doesn't mean we shouldn't try! I am convinced that too often we quickly decide that we know our students. Cumulative file, some diagnostic testing, cursory observation, and a parent-teacher conference here and there, and presto! we know our students.

But then suddenly we run into children like Keith, whom we thought we knew, at least well enough to conclude that he is an incorrigible brat. Then we realize that there is much more to the lives of these students than meets the eye.

The principles at issue, Lisa, are these: we must (1) teach the *whole* child, and (2) recognize that every child has a unique set of gifts and needs. These two principles taken together require that (a) we indeed must seek to know, as far as we can, the whole child—not just his academic achievement or a catalog of behavior problems—and that (b) we try to make it possible to celebrate his or her unique gifts and meet his or her special needs. Note that these principles are correlatives. You need the one in order to work with the other. Only when we know the whole child is it possible that we come to understand a wide range of gifts and needs; and only when we strive to identify and capitalize on all of a child's gifts, including those that at first glance seem irrelevant to your specific lessons, only then can we do justice to, and teach, the whole child.

Teachers should take considerable time at the beginning of the term to do extensive inventory work. Yes, you need to know some of the stuff you will find in the cumulative file, of course. But be careful with the cumulative file in any case, as it can prejudice you. Make sure to go beyond such documents. What is this child *really* like? Does he have a dominant learning style? Who is his family and what is his social background? Who are his friends? What does she judge to be some of the most important experiences of her life? What are his hobbies? What is she good at? What does she dislike? What priorities shape her life? What are his hopes and his fears? Her dreams? How does the child feel about the Lord?

I recognize that we must be careful with the use of questionnaires and surveys. There are right-to-privacy laws, and some of our inventory work may be interpreted as prying. If you were to ask your students how well their parents are getting along with each other, you may soon receive some telephone calls, first from an irate parent and then from the principal! So our questions and surveys must be done with Christian sensitivity, not out of morbid curiosity. And, of course, always remember that responses to questionnaires are to be voluntary.

Is it too late in the school year for such inventories? At any time of the year there are opportunities to inquire, to explore, and to learn about the lives of your students. If you are not sure about gifts and needs, design some activities that will help you find out. Offer children not only a diversity of ways in which they demonstrate their learning, but also give them a wide range of options for disclosing their lives to you, from writing autobiographies and stories about their favorite heroes to asking them to build their dream home or perfect little islands in the sea. Tie your teaching, as much as possible, into the lives of the students. Don't hesitate to ask them for suggestions.

I also encourage you to seize opportunities to get to know your students outside of the structured classroom context. Attend their special events such as recitals or ballgames. Maybe you can spend some time hiking with your students or camping with them. Don't turn down invitations to visit the homes of your students, and consider inviting your students to visit your home. Take the children out for a pizza lunch or to a sporting event. All these activities will enhance your understanding of the children you are teaching.

The recurring questions, you must ask, Lisa, are these: How well do I really know my students? What can I do to learn more about them? What really makes them tick? You must ask such questions of *every one* of your students, not just of the bright ones or the behavior problems. Each of your children is precious in the eyes of the Lord. Every one of them is worth knowing—and loving. Even Keith!

Keep me posted, okay?

Dad

11

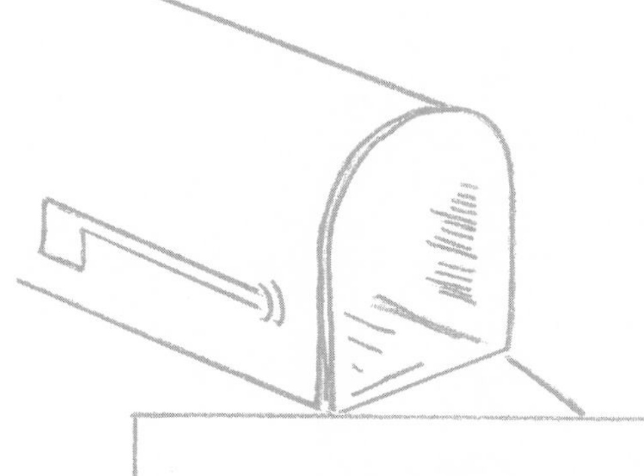

Are my assessment and grading practices compatible with teaching Christianly?

Subject: The agony of grading
From: Lisa
To: Dad
Date: Fri, 17 Nov 16:37:02 -0800 (PST)

Hi Dad,

Well, another round of parent-teacher conferences! I must tell you, Dad, that I was shocked by one mother whose primary concern seemed to be whether her boy was doing A or "merely" B work. I guess she expects her son to become President of the United States some day, so he must get all A's! Whether or not the kid is learning anything seems immaterial to her. And how her son gets along with other children or with himself does not appear to matter much to her either.

I reminded this parent—I tried to be gentle!—that, contrary to popular opinion, grades are not the most important indicators of what or how well children are learning. Like this parent, even some of my colleagues seem to view grades as bottom-line benchmarks. They equate evaluation with grading, even though in college it was stamped into our heads that we need to distinguish sharply between grading/reporting on the one hand, and evaluating/assessment on the other. I remember your saying once that as soon as we identify evaluation with grading, or assume the crazy proposition that we evaluate in order to give and report grades, we lose the heart of what it means to teach Christianly.

This whole evaluation and grading business, Dad, frustrates me to no end. I think it's the worst part of teaching! Any thoughts on the matter?

Love, Lisa

Friday, November 17

Dear Lisa,

Yes, I recognize the agony of evaluation and grading. We've aggravated the agony because, as you say, too often grades have become bottom-line benchmarks—a very unfortunate condition. Nevertheless, I think you will agree that evaluation is endemic to all good teaching, including good Christian teaching. As teachers we need to work constantly at evaluating whether our students are really learning what we want them to learn, and we need to continually evaluate our own teaching practice. But we must make sure we evaluate what we value and not the other way around. And if our students are not learning, we should not conclude that they are dummies. Instead, we should ask: How could I adjust my teaching? If one of our students does not seem motivated, we should not say: What an ungrateful, unmotivated kid! Instead, we ask: Why is this child unmotivated? Is there something in his background I don't know about? Is it my teaching? What am I doing that I should not be doing or vice versa? This kind of careful, frank evaluation needs constant attention and cultivation.

Though to some it may sound like technical gibberish, I do believe it is useful to make another distinction: between evaluation and assessment. Assessment refers to the *means* of evaluation, the "collecting of data," as the textbooks somewhat ostentatiously put it. Careful observation of our students, for example, is a type of assessment: it gives us a basis for evaluation. Writing assignments, students' products, some testing, and various types of performances are means of evaluation. They are all assessment techniques. Assessment helps us understand what students know and how they learn most effectively. With the data we collect we can evaluate the students and determine what they need to learn next and the support we can give them in their learning.

Now it seems to me that evaluation and assessment are necessary and not overly problematic. Of course, we can go overboard by excessive concentration on testing. Tests or quizzes should be used sparingly lest we encourage the "teaching/learning for the test" syndrome. I was dismayed the other day to hear a child in a fourth grade I visited ask the all-too-familiar question: "Teacher, will this be on the test?" Already for that youngster real learning has deteriorated into a mere hoop to jump through. I suspect you have such children in your fifth-grade class, don't you, Lisa? They present you with the hefty challenge of trying to deprogram them!

The real problem emerges, however, when we look at our grading practices. Grading basically means to assign a numerical quantity to student work. It was introduced in the industrial age when employers needed to sort workers into classes. Workers were graded the way eggs are graded: good, mediocre, and rejected. Unfortunately, the practice of grading has stuck. I say unfortunately because this sorting and ranking business—called "normative grading"—inevitably produces winners and losers. Do you see what I mean? Normative grading is really a sorting and ranking mechanism; it always means comparing children with each other: some will inevitably do better than others. Some will get good grades, some will not. Some will make the grade, others lose out. Normative grading loudly proclaims: there is no way that all students can succeed! Now ask yourself as a Christian teacher: Can I be happy with a system that forces me to see some of the children in my class as failures even before I have actually met them?

Grading understood as sorting and ranking—which is how the students, too, understand it—introduces unwelcome competition, at least for a while. May the best man win, that is, may the best students get the coveted A, and never mind the rest. For a while the rest may be motivated to match the success of the A students; but once it becomes clear to them that the lines are hard to cross, they give up. This is one reason why grading is singularly unhelpful to both the student and the teacher.

I remember how, as a high school teacher, I experienced the profound agony of having to grade. In my tenth-grade English class I had to teach a unit on grammar. I remember students like

Norman and Dean, who already knew their grammar cold. They got A after A on their assignments without trying. But then there were students like Loren and Dick. They tried and tried and struggled and struggled, but just could not get it. Now I see what I did not clearly understand at that time 30 years ago: these students were blessed with differing learning styles; my teaching of grammar was clearly geared to the analytic and sequential learning style of Norman and Dean. Loren and Dick were left in the dust. In spite of all the special help I provided, they got D after D, until they finally gave up.

Did my grading of these students' work help or hinder their learning? This, after all, is the fundamental question. If grades actually help students learn, well, let's keep them. But if they hinder, should we not get rid of them?

Already back in my days as a high school teacher I could see that my grading practice did nothing to help Norman and Dean learn. They got their A's easily, without doing much work. They merely—and dutifully—demonstrated what they already knew. No learning was required. The A's actually deterred them from doing any more than meet the basic requirements. Why do more? Is there life beyond an A?

Similarly, the discouraging D did nothing to solve Loren and Dick's problem. They finally gave up. Why try when there is no chance for success? Of course, I should have considered different teaching strategies. But even then, I'm sure, grading would not have been helpful.

I recall from one of our earlier conversations, Lisa, that you feel grades attach labels to the students. Once a child is identified as a D student, his chances for success are seriously diminished. Especially in some of the smaller schools, where students move through the grade levels together, the "dummies" have no chance of escape.

Well, Lisa, what are you going to do about this grading mess? Join the ranks of teachers who complain about grading but can't do a thing about it? I am afraid that many teachers feel forced to choose this option. And, yes, as long as there are bells, 40-minute class periods, and standardized tests, we probably will have grading. Nevertheless, there are encouraging signs to the contrary. Increasing numbers of educators, parents, and business people are raising serious questions about the meaningfulness of grading. Even national news magazines and TV reports are raising the issues. I am sure, Lisa, that some day new systems of assessment and reporting will win the day. But heaps of things will have to change first.

So what can you do in the meantime? Let me challenge you to creatively seek to minimize the problem. And, indeed, there are some things you can do. For example, systematically begin to cut back on your grading. I mean, don't feel obliged to attach a grade to every piece of work your students do for you, in spite of their protests or demands. Of course, do give plenty of feedback. Remember, evaluation is supposed to help students learn, not lock them up in cast-iron boxes. And postpone summative grades as long as you can. Allow your students to try again and again. I know, it may mean even more planning and paper work and time. You will have to judge what you can do without working yourself into a frenzy. But it is important that you wean your students away from the notion that they are essentially working for grades. This, of course, is one of the greatest problems with grades: it encourages students to work for reward, not for the activity—learning, in this case—that leads to a reward. As Alfie Kohn and others point out, grades (and other rewards) demean and belittle the work required for the reward.

I also suggest you pick up on the current interest in portfolios. A collection of items produced by the students over a period of time will do much more to help us understand a student's progress than a set of cold, unexplained grades. Consider working together with your colleagues on collecting useful student portfolios. Along with this type of assessment, be sure to establish programs of self-evaluation. Have the students set learning goals and help them to develop criteria for evaluating themselves. And always emphasize student growth and success. Point to what they actually learned, rather than to what they failed to learn.

When you absolutely must grade, Lisa, then do keep the child in mind. Remember, we are dealing with precious image-bearers of God, not eggs. So be very careful. Always be able to explain the grades you assign. And don't use lines such as "this kid deserves an A" or "this kid deserves an F" and the like. Our evaluation of students is always approximate, never absolute. We bring into the process our own strengths and weaknesses, our own prejudices, our own learning styles, and our personal feelings. We never understand our students well enough to be sure of total accuracy, objective tests notwithstanding. And when we must assign a low grade, there is always the nagging question: Did I really do everything possible to help this child? Could it be that I am partly to blame for the student's failure to learn?

In your own quiet way, attempt to make your own classroom such an exciting place for learning that for both students and parents the need for grades begins to fade into the background. Instead, let satisfaction arise from what students have discovered or learned to do.

Dad

12

What about competition in my classroom?

Dec. 6

Hi Dad,

My class is out for P.E., and I should be looking at my lesson plans for the rest of the day, but I just feel it's important to scribble a note to you. I'll put it in the mail here at school before I leave for the day. You know, just a little while ago you and I talked about grading. Well, I discussed this with a colleague and suggested that normative grading—sorting and ranking, you called it—creates a competitive rather than a collaborative environment.

But Dad, I'm just not sure I agree with you that a competitive classroom environment is always a bad thing. Doesn't competition motivate students to do their best and to achieve? Look at those athletes, for example. Doesn't tough competition lead to marvelous successes? And what about that big cruel dog-eat-dog world out there! Shouldn't we provide plenty of practice so our kids will be equipped to handle all that competition? Why, even the Apostle Paul commends competition. In I Corinthians 9 he tells us: "Do you not know that in a race all the runners run, but only one gets the prize? Run in such a way as to get the prize." If that isn't competition, what is?

Well, I'll leave it at that. I challenge you to a competition of ideas!

Love,

Lisa

Wednesday, December 13

Dear Lisa,

You are asking some important questions. How, do you suppose, Christians would respond? They would probably line up on different sides of the competition debate. Some of them will respond, "Amen, sister" to your suggestion that competition is healthy and leads to greater achievement. Others are not so sure. They worry about the excessive emphasis some schools put on sports and on other sorts of competition, from spelling bees to honor rolls. They are concerned about the children who inevitably lose such contests. There are even those who applaud and endorse authors like Alfie Kohn, who vigorously argues that any form of competition shuts down learning and hurts everyone, including the winners and losers.

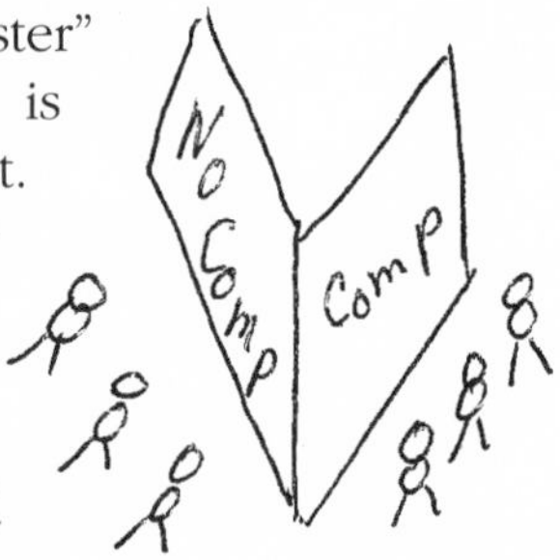

Well, what do you think, Lisa? On what bandwagon do you want to ride? "Ah, but Dad," I hear you say, "I don't want to join any bandwagon—these bandwagons get stuck in ruts pretty fast, especially when they declare their position to be the only one that's right. Why not choose a middle way, condemn excesses, and stay tuned to other options?"

Okay, I hear you. But let's be sure we understand why we are choosing a middle way. And we need to figure out whether our position might be right or left of center. Unexamined positions, even when they appear to be in the middle, tend to drift quickly to the extremes.

So what guiding principles can we propose? I suggest we begin with the Scriptures. Do we really find models of competition, approved of God, in the Bible? Can we find places that encourage either the process of competition or the result of competition (namely, winning)? Look again at the passage you quote from Corinthians. In the verse that follows (I Cor. 9:25) Paul says: "Everyone who competes in the games goes into strict training. They do it to get a crown that will not last; but we do it to get a crown that will last forever." Does this not suggest that Paul has a rather low opinion of competing in games? After all, competing in games will only win a temporary crown. If we compete at all, Paul says, it is to win a lasting crown. What sort of competition brings us to such a lasting crown? Winning, so we can be the best? No, rather, we must outdo each other in love. We must strive to serve the other. We should eagerly seek not our own good, but the good of others (I Cor. 10:24). If we want to excel at all, let us excel in gifts that build up others (I Cor. 14:12).

The truth is that competition always involves efforts to be better than or superior to someone else. It always involves coming out ahead of others. But that sort of picture is foreign to the biblical message of love, servanthood, and esteeming others better than ourselves. The biblical view depicts people who want *others* to be better than themselves. They want to step back so that others may win, yes, so that *everyone* may win. Ultimately the message is this: when we allow others to win—in the right sense of the word—we allow God Himself to win.

So much for the sermon! It would be easy to haul out a bagful of Bible texts to support what I have just said. But I do not want to land us in a verse-slinging battle. Then we'd be stuck in another sort of contest: who can quote the largest number of texts for or against competition!

It is interesting to note, though, that more and more research supports the conclusion that, in general, competition in the classroom is not a good thing. A bit here and there, as in some games, may be okay. It provides variety. But even in the "harmless" forms of competition there appears to lurk some danger. Good students, for example, like the competition because it allows them to shine. But such "shining" is problematic: for such students the "shining" becomes the goal, the winning and excelling, while what they have to do to win becomes less important. The crucial thing is the reward, not the activity leading to the reward.

Meanwhile, even in "harmless competition" those who lose stand to lose more than just a game. Losing is tough, even under ideal circumstances. Yes, I know, we will have to learn to be "good losers." But there is no evidence that experience at losing produces "good losers." On the contrary, the more we lose the less we think of ourselves and the more we are tempted to quit. Experience with losing produces losers, not good losers.

Think of your class, Lisa. I know you have the children play plenty of games, and I do not object to that practice. I also know you fully understand the important distinction between matched and unmatched competition. Unmatched competition is as unfair as expecting a person with one leg in a cast to jump as high as the star athlete. Clearly, there can be no place for unmatched competition in a Christian classroom. Yet I often see such unmatched competition, even in Christian schools.

Take the commonly played round-the-world math game. It is a classic example of unmatched competition. In this game the top math students compete with the bottom and middle within the same time frame. The middle and bottom students don't have a ghost of a chance, unless they cheat somehow. The "mad minute" math facts worksheet presents similar problems.

One of the most pernicious forms of unmatched competition is the timed standardized achievement test. Even though such tests are touted as fair, since they presumably give equal chance to all, in reality they viciously discriminate against those students whose learning style, if they are to be successful, requires the sort of relaxed time frames and environment that such tests do not provide.

One way of keeping competition matched is to have mixed ability groups play a game together. At least, one would think that such mixed groups have an equal chance at success. Still, I have seen problems here. One is that at times a team messes up because of a mistake or the ineptitude of one single team member. That student, consequently, becomes a target of scorn—sometimes silent, unspoken scorn.

The more I observe classrooms, the more I doubt whether "matched competition" is even possible. What do you think? You believe in the uniqueness of each child, don't you? Does that not suggest that no two people, not even two teams, are ever evenly matched?

Well, Lisa, I don't know whether these remarks help or hinder. Getting back to the bandwagons: I advise you to be extremely skeptical of any claim that supports the use of competition in the classroom. Rather, I advise you to continue to work on establishing a collaborative classroom, a place in which your students can practice servanthood and self-effacing love—concepts admittedly not popular in our self-seeking, winner-takes-all, materialistic world. But I have gone on long enough. I look forward to seeing you next weekend when you come home for Christmas break. Let's continue the conversation at that time, okay?

Dad

13

Is cooperative learning a Christian strategy?

Subject: Cooperative learning
From: Lisa
To: Dad
Date: Mon, 8 Jan 16:03:25 -0800 (PST)

Hi Dad,

Guess what! I have decided to get into cooperative learning. Whole hog! I mean, cooperative learning in the technical sense. As you know, I have always done a lot of group work. I have the kids get into groups where they work together and help each other. But I think you call this "simply group work" or some such thing, right? Just putting kids into groups is not really cooperative learning. Cooperative learning, as I understand it, means that you structure a group activity in such a way that no single group member can complete a task without input from all the other group members. "Positive interdependence" it is called, right?

Anyway, we had a staff meeting this afternoon to talk about cooperative learning. The principal came out in strong support of the idea. He quoted some research that shows that cooperative learning, if done right, produces better learning and reduces discipline problems. But the staff is not agreed on this thing. One teacher stood up and declared that cooperative learning is a fad, eventually destined for the educational trash heap, like all the other fads. Another one said that cooperative learning is unchristian because it leads to relativism, or something like that. She believes that cooperative learning is the result of New Age thinking. But I agree with the principal, Dad, at least enough to try it. Why, do you think, are some staff members scared of cooperative learning?

Love, Lisa

Monday evening, January 8

Dear Lisa,

You ask an interesting and important question: Why do some teachers regard cooperative learning as an intimidating, scary sort of thing, or maybe even a thoroughly unchristian approach to teaching? Well, maybe here is the answer: Put yourself in the shoes of some of these teachers. They have been teaching for years in more traditional, tried-and-tested modes. They have managed to do quite a good job: students learn, parents are satisfied with the report cards, and classroom discipline has been no problem at all. So why change?

Now here comes this newfangled stuff about cooperative learning. What is the skeptic's response? His or her line of thinking might go somewhat as follows:

Now I have to start planning for weird structures like heterogeneous groups, positive interdependence, and processing. Worse, now I have to set up classrooms in which the kids are *encouraged* to do a lot of talking, after years of trying to get them to do just the opposite: to be quiet and listen to me! So what will happen? I can picture these kids in small groups yakking a mile a minute. I can see what's going to happen: plenty of off-task behavior, goofing off, and discipline problems. This cooperative learning stuff obviously leads to a pack of trouble.

In addition, what are the parents of my students going to say? I can hear them now: "What's going on in your class, pray tell? I hear you're wasting a lot of time by having the kids rap together, pool their ignorance, and generally learn nothing! Besides, what's the idea of having your students prattle to see what the truth might be? Don't you realize that we Christians *have* the truth, and that—as Deuteronomy tells us once and for all—we are to *imprint* the truth on the impressionable minds of these youngsters?"

I predict that parents would blast me with strong reactions. Plus the parents of very bright kids could have additional complaints. I can just hear Mr. Otis: "What? Are you asking my

Steve to waste his valuable time making sure that the slow ones in his cooperative learning group can pass? Listen here, I'm paying a fortune to have my kid educated. I want you to *teach* him at *his* pace, you hear? That's what you're getting paid for!"

Is this what some of your friends may be thinking, Lisa? I would not be surprised. And in some ways I cannot blame them. We tend to be creatures of habit. Don't we feel more comfortable when we walk home on the same side of the street every time? As you well know, teaching very much involves *style*. We teach long enough, and eventually we fall into a set of recognizable habits, a recognizable style with which we feel very comfortable. We will resist any new approach that might nudge us out of our style and will try to rationalize it away as a fad.

I know enough about you as a person and a teacher, Lisa, to sense that the arguments just proposed by the critical skeptic do not hold much water for you. You are one to strike out in new directions, to see if you can improve on your already considerably successful style of teaching Christianly. You are willing to "style-flex," to borrow a term from the learning style theorists. And I'm glad of it. I am glad that you are willing to give cooperative learning your very best shot.

As you think about your teaching approaches, Lisa, let me remind you of a crucial distinction, the distinction between cooperative learning and a collaborative classroom. I have written to you before on the nature of a collaborative classroom. I think I did so at the time we were discussing competition and different kinds of classroom atmospheres. Remember, the collaborative classroom is the *context* in which you do your teaching. It is the environment you create—even if you were never to use any technically correct cooperative learning teaching strategies. The difference between the collaborative classroom and cooperative learning is a little bit like the difference between the ballpark and the ballgame. The game can be played in different ways with different strategies, but the ballpark remains the ballpark.

Cooperative learning, then, is simply one specific strategy, one that is extremely useful for establishing and maintaining a collaborative classroom. But it is only *one* strategy. It may not even be an indispensable strategy. Although I have to do some more thinking about this, I do believe that a collaborative classroom does not depend on cooperative learning strategies. The opposite, however, appears to be false: while a collaborative classroom does not always require technically precise cooperative learning strategies, cooperative learning, to be really effective, does require the context of a collaborative classroom.

I must emphasize this point. We easily fall into the trap of implementing group learning strategies without adequate attention to the larger collaborative classroom atmosphere. I mean, so often I see teachers who run basically individualistic, even competitive classrooms, then from 2:00 to 3:00 in the afternoon introduce some cooperative learning. But what kinds of mixed messages will students get? If they compete in the morning and have no concern about each other's learning until noon, what good will a cooperative learning session in the early afternoon do?

Of course, *some* well-designed cooperative learning is better than none at all. After all, whenever we can get children to cooperate, help each other, and serve each other, we are meeting some of the demands of the Lord. Whenever we have opportunity to create community, let's seize the moment. But unless from the very beginning you intend to turn your classroom into a real collaborative classroom, do not expect some scattered cooperative learning activity here and there to bring about a caring classroom community.

I'm curious about what definitions/descriptions of cooperative learning your principal shared with you. As a Christian, I am comfortable with some theorists and not others. I would be careful with, for instance, some of the programs of Robert Slavin at Johns Hopkins. There tends to be quite a bit of behaviorism there. Be sure to study the literature about these things. Compare Slavin's work, for example, with that of the Johnson brothers at the University of Minnesota. Spencer Kagan's stuff is also worth looking at and will give you food for thought. Do you have their books available in your staff library? If not, strongly suggest them to your principal! This material should be required reading for every Christian teacher.

I have tried to persuade you to distinguish not only between a collaborative classroom and cooperative learning, but also between cooperative learning and "simply group work." The short of it is that cooperative learning involves some very specific techniques. One of them is the forming of heterogeneous groups. That means that you carefully select the composition of every group. As a general rule, groups should be a mixture of boys and girls, as ethnically diverse as possible, and representative of different ability levels. Don't allow the students to choose their own groups! On the basis of your knowledge of the class, *you* decide on the make-up of the groups. Incidentally, try to form groups of even numbers. Groups of four work best. If you have groups of three, two of the group members may bond, while the third one will be the "odd man out." And once you form the groups, keep them together for a month or two; it takes time to become attuned to each other and to learn to work together.

Another key principle in cooperative learning is "positive interdependence." This means that when you assign a group task, no single member can complete the task without input from all the others, or, to put it conversely, every group member needs the assistance of every other group member in order to complete the task. You can achieve such interdependence in several ways. One is to assign roles: one member is a reader, another a reporter, another a prober or critic, or a checker, a taskmaster, noise monitor, or whatever. Another way is to divide the task into parts so that each member has control of and responsibility for one part and needs to contribute to the group in order to bring the project to completion. Suppose your lesson is on the industrial revolution. You could ask group members to take responsibility for different aspects of this bit of history. Some could study the religious background of the revolution, others the social factors, and still others the political and economic background. Then they could all come together, share, teach one another, and be accountable for their own and each other's learning.

Cooperative learning specialists talk a lot about "processing." This term refers to communal reflection on how well the group has worked together. It is a crucial, even indispensable component. After the group activity, have the students write or talk together as they evaluate their group work, identifying weaknesses and committing themselves to improving next time around.

But you can read about these matters in the literature, Lisa. I don't need to provide chapter and verse. The important point to acknowledge is that these strategies are eminently compatible with teaching Christianly. Cooperative learning fosters community, allows students to practice discipleship skills, and encourages them to take responsibility for their own and each other's learning. My regret is that we Christians had to wait for the secular world to discover the basic principles. We ourselves should have researched and articulated this kind of classroom approach. We should have developed both the theory and the practice of truly communal, caring, and effective cooperative education. We should have taken our findings and proclaimed them to the world at large. Our message should have been: This is a way of teaching and learning which pleases the Lord, helps students learn, and brings about mutual acceptance, peace, and healing.

Once again, Lisa, I'm glad to hear of your enthusiasm. Go to it, and let me know how it turns out, okay?

Dad

14

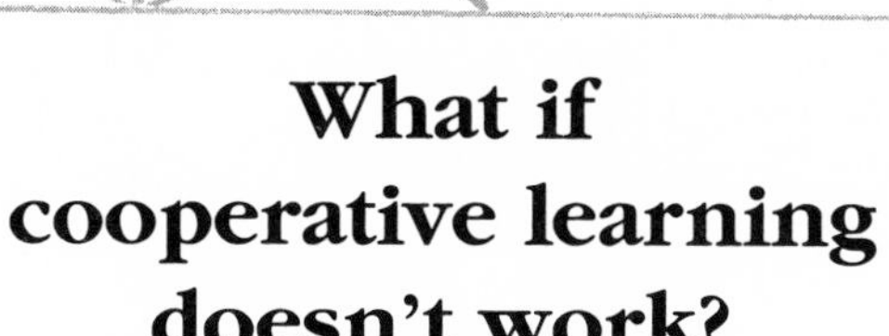

What if cooperative learning doesn't work?

Subject: Coop learning—a bomb!
From: Lisa
To: Dad
Date: Tue, 23 Jan 15:30:53 -0800 (PST)

Hi Dad,

Well, I've tried cooperative learning, and I tell you the truth: It doesn't work! Nothing but problems. I find that my cooperative learning groups turn out to be "simply group work." In one group especially, loudmouth Keith—sorry to sound bitter—takes charge and practically runs the whole show. That is not cooperation—that's plain bullying. And in another group Marci simply refuses to participate. She is kind of a sullen kid anyway, and she says she hates to work with others. She can do the work much faster and much better on her own, she claims.

And, really, Dad, I did set up the groups according to the rules: I put four in a group, mixed them up, and made sure they sat facing each other. I even kept the groups away from the wall so the kids wouldn't lean back and tune out! And I separated the groups far enough from each other so that I could walk a complete circle around each one of them. And I thought it would be a great idea to allow the groups to choose team names. But this tactic, too, only primed the competition pumps. All the kids wanted to do is compete with each other. I'm frustrated and discouraged, Dad! In fact, I'm about to chuck the whole thing.

Help!

Love, Lisa

Subject: Re: Coop learning—a bomb!
From: Dad
To: Lisa
Date: Tue, 23 Jan 19:08:21 -0600 (CST)

Dear Lisa,

I was surprised to hear from you so soon after you wrote me about your plans to go for cooperative learning whole hog. I thought you would give it more time, more of a chance than you did. You have barely begun to implement the strategy, and already you're admitting defeat!

Let me sound an encouraging note. We may have overlooked one very important ingredient in this cooperative learning business, namely, the expectations you set before you introduce your first cooperative learning lessons. I'm somewhat rushed right now, so I'll write you a letter about this ingredient a little bit later.

Dad

Wednesday, January 24

Dear Lisa,

As I suggested in my e-mail message, cooperative learning strategies are difficult to implement without first paying plenty of attention to the expectations you set. Of course, setting expectations for your class is absolutely essential for whatever teaching strategy you use. Such expectations consist of two large areas: first, what you expect your students to learn, and, secondly, how you expect them to relate to each other in the classroom (I prefer to put it this way, rather than merely how you expect the children to behave). At the beginning of the year you discussed your goals and objectives with your class, right? And you have a set of rules on the wall. Come to think of it, in your classroom you have posted only two rules, if I recall. Something like "Do nothing unhelpful" and "Be very kind to everyone." These rules were actually proposed by your students, I believe, rather than simply imposed on the class.

But when you initiate cooperative learning procedures, Lisa, it becomes particularly important to articulate, review, and practice the specific discipleship skills you and your students have agreed to display. The literature about cooperative learning talks about this too, and usually refers to such skills as "social skills." But I think we are talking about more than merely barebones social skills, don't you agree? We are looking at very specific ways in which the fruit of the Spirit is to be evidenced and practiced. Discipleship skills include "social skills" but extend far beyond them to address all sorts of relationships with ourselves, our fellow human beings, the entire creation, and the Lord himself. You need to guide the students in spelling out these skills and encourage the children to take ownership of them. You need to teach the children to accept accountability for them.

This discipling is no easy task. We know that sin "cleaves to us" everywhere, as an old church formulary puts it, and that by nature we are selfish, greedy, and "prone to hate God and neighbor."

Still, if we as teachers are not willing to address this situation head-on, we will always stumble along and thereby invite even greater frustrations, especially when we conduct cooperative learning lessons. I generally advise teachers to begin with the easy discipleship skills, the ones that all children know about and understand. For example, showing respect for others. Kids immediately understand what this means when you state the opposite: no put-downs. Incidentally, it is always a good idea to discuss with your class both the positive and negative manifestations of a given discipleship skill.

Let's just talk about this respect thing. You have, on occasion, shared with me your disappointment at the disrespect displayed by children from Christian families. Seasoned principals and teachers tell me that they observe a continuing decline of respect on the part of students. You must deal with this problem in a forthright manner. Already you have modeled respect for each one of your students, I am sure, even to the point where you say "Thank you" when children respond to your questions. Now, before you start cooperative learning lessons, hold a general class discussion. Brainstorm the ways in which the children can show respect and ways in which they show disrespect. Write them out on the chalkboard. Then have the children do some skits in which they demonstrate both put-downs and respect. Read a gripping story about a youngster who fails to be respectful. Teach them how to respond when others are disrespectful to them. And have the children concretely practice respectful behavior, following their own explicit guidelines and unmistakable examples.

At first such practice may look artificial to you and to the class. But the fact is, children often do what they first practice. They may even come to like the practiced behavior. It is a little bit like learning to swim. I remember my own swimming lessons back in the Netherlands. As a little boy I was hung in a wide leather strap on a pole above the water and instructed to practice the breast stroke. I felt awkward and silly. But soon it became second nature, so that even today I can swim almost as effortlessly as I can walk.

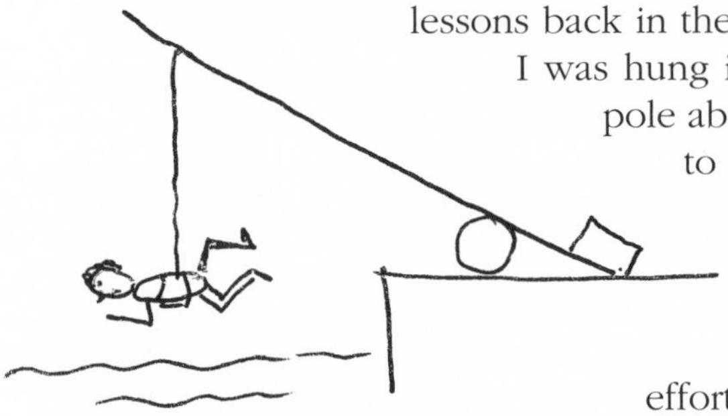

Of course I am not so naive as to think that these rehearsals will solve all your problems, Lisa. Of course not. But not deliberately working at these skills will invite more problems and make matters worse.

It is a good idea to single out specific discipleship skills—or servanthood skills—every week. Post them as the "discipleship skill of the week." Take encouragement, for example. This is an important skill and requires much discussion, modeling, and practice. One teacher I know taught his students encouragement by first deliberately discouraging them in a sustained way. He had the kids do a project and every time they would show it to him and the class, he would slam them to the wall, as it were. "What's the matter with you guys?" he would shout. "Can't you do anything right? What kind of shoddy work is this?" And so on. When finally the students were getting quite perturbed, even angry, about such obviously unfair critique, the teacher stopped everything and said: "Now let's talk about what has been happening here." From then on he easily and effectively reminded his students to be encouraging by simply referring to this episode. I realize that to some this may seem like a questionable strategy, one that could easily backfire. But I am trying to make a point.

Well, Lisa, you get the idea. In the rush to cover the material and get the curriculum taught, it is easy to neglect developing such skills. And there are plenty such skills to be concerned about. I think of listening to one another, helping each other, treating each other with respect, letting the other person be first, accepting differences, and so on. Earlier I referred to the fruit of the Spirit. Paul talks about it in numerous places in his letters. For you and your class a study of these passages will be no idle exercise. These passages apply directly to you and your students as you work together at teaching and learning.

Together. That reminds us of the core of the issue at hand. I mean, if you are going to get your class to be collaborative and if you want to succeed at cooperative learning, you are going to have to put a lot of pizzazz into the idea of "togetherness." Not cozy, schmaltzy, warm fuzzies, but a real sense of hey! this is *our* classroom—not just a classroom run by the teacher for obedient, compliant children, but a place where the youngsters are participants, not just recipients. It is a place where the students have some ownership and are given meaningful responsibilities.

No, Lisa, I am not daydreaming about a Deweyan democracy of yesteryear. Of course not. You are the teacher, an office bearer appointed to be a teacher by almighty God himself, invested with authority and responsibility. You remain the guide. But exercising authority responsibly means to exercise servant leadership: not an I'm-the-boss-do-as-I-say kind of authoritarianism, but a firm, gentle, caring guidance. So give the children room to maneuver, to make choices, and to share responsibility with you.

That brings me back to expectations again. It is one thing to tell the students, "I want you to be nice to each other or else!" It is quite another to have them purposefully decide, right along with you, that they will indeed be nice to one another. Have them agree just what it means to be nice, and what consequences should follow when they fail to live up to their agreement. In this way you get the students to covenant together. Teachers and students covenant, in trust and fairness, to relate to one another in positive, helpful, constructive ways.

Of course, such a covenant can be fostered only if you encourage the students to really get to know each other. Many of them do, of course, but often their knowledge of each other is superficial and colored by peer-painted glasses. Here you might review my letter on getting to know students, if you still have it. What applied to the teacher applies to the students as well.

I hope you will continue to experiment with cooperative learning strategies—there are so many helpful ones—and especially concentrate on teaching discipleship skills. Let's keep reminding each other—and our students—that learning and knowledge and skills mean little or nothing without the greatest discipleship skill of them all: love!

I look forward to receiving more stories from your classroom.

Dad

15

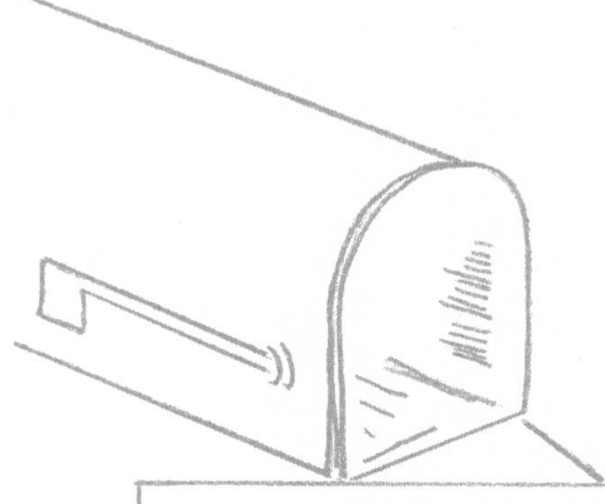

How can I meet students' needs in my classroom?

Saturday, February 3

Dear Lisa,

There was good news and bad news in your recent letter. The good news is that your school is flourishing, like the grass after a spring rain. Student enrollment is up, and staff morale is high, especially since the board voted to increase your salaries substantially. The bad news is that it looks as if your class size will substantially increase as well. Looking at the number of fourth-graders now, and assuming no staffing changes, you can count on more than 30 students in your class next fall. How will you will be able to meet the needs of all those children next year? Already you feel overwhelmed with the 27 you are responsible for right now.

You have plenty of reasons to feel overwhelmed. At least 27 of them! And your students, too, have reason to feel that way. I am sure—and I think you are, too—that the needs of many of them are not met in your classroom, in spite of your best efforts. And most likely not all of their gifts are recognized and celebrated. Plenty of hidden talents probably remain well hidden!

Large class size is one of the most serious and frustrating structural problems we teachers face. Combine this problem with the unrelenting shortage of time, and you *know* that teaching Christianly is going to be seriously compromised. Under these conditions we begin to cut corners and look for shortcuts in our pedagogy, evaluation procedures, and personal reflections. And the students suffer; at the least, they are significantly shortchanged.

Money is always cited as the main reason for oversized classes. Economic realities appear to leave no other options. Frankly, I am always skeptical of such an argument. I suspect the problem may have more to do with parental priorities and financial management.

Whatever the causes, the reality remains: You will have no shortage of children to teach next year. As you indicated in your letter, you recognize your moral obligation here. Since the Lord created each one of those 30 plus children unique and special, it is your moral obligation to meet, as best as you can, the needs of each one of them. You have no right to say to the Lord: "Sorry, I know I have to teach different kids with different needs and different gifts, but I can't pay much attention to this; I am going to treat them as if they are all alike. It's a lot less stressful that way. And be realistic, Lord: How could I possibly meet the needs of each one of these kids? After all, you put only 24 hours in a day!"

Remember, Lisa, even if there were only half a dozen in your class, you *still* could not meet all the needs. Children are simply too complicated. And so the question is, how can I do the best possible job, given the complex nature of the children, the large number in my class, and ever-present time constraints?

One thing *not* to do, it seems to me, is to do what we teachers generally and often unconsciously do. We reduce the diversity in the class to three basic categories: the low achievers, the high achievers, and the "kids in the middle." Both the low and the high achievers get your attention pretty quickly. The low achievers struggle and fuss, while the high achievers sail along. Both types bring along peculiar management problems, but that is a discussion we shall postpone until another time.

The "kids in the middle," meanwhile, probably form the largest group. They are, at least outwardly, a homogeneous collection of "average kids." They don't stand out one way or another. They blend together, as it were.

Actually, these "kids in the middle" are the ones who are short-changed the most. You see why, don't you? Well, the gifts of the high achievers are often recognized, and, as a result, they benefit from various acceleration and enrichment programs. The low achievers, too, are easily identified and receive special attention in the form of remedial programs and special education services. But what about the "kids in the middle"? Their needs, and their gifts, often go undetected.

Well, what can I do? I can hear you ask the question. I think, Lisa, that you would do well to consider planning a three-pronged program for next year. It won't solve all the problems, but at least it will help. And it may alleviate your sense of frustration. Your frustration and stress will be reduced when you know you have done all you can.

Okay, so let's take a look at this three-pronged program. The first prong consists of a careful plan to inventory your new students at the beginning of the fall term. The important thing is to learn as much as you can about your students, especially so that you can identify the gifts and needs of *every one* of your students, not just those whom the cumulative files indicate to be high or low achievers.

What do you suppose are gifts and needs in the first place? How can we describe them? Here our overarching goal of leading into discipleship comes into play again. Gifts, I believe, are all those factors that enhance a student's ability to serve God and his neighbor. Needs are all those factors that detract from such ability. Gifts and needs, like breakfast cereals, come in all varieties and all sizes.

So think not only of academic gifts or learning needs, Lisa, but consider aesthetic, social, and emotional gifts and needs as well. You might think of Howard Gardner's multiple intelligences at this point. And don't forget about spiritual needs. Try to discover the relationship—or absence thereof—between the students and the Lord.

I suggest you design a variety of activities at the beginning of the term that will help you identify gifts and needs. Then, at the least, you will have something to work on. Be sure to include activities that allow the shy youngsters to shine. Give students opportunity to discuss and display hands-on learning, creative talents, and social graces. Also see to it that they can talk about their hobbies and interests. These are good indicators of a child's talents.

The second prong of your plan to meet the needs and celebrate the gifts of all your students, including those of the "kids in the middle," is to take another look at your curriculum. From the very start, think of it as a "multiple-opportunity" curriculum. Decide what it is you want all your students to know. Call this the core curriculum, if you will. Then ask yourself, how can I add activities that will allow the high achievers to advance according to their abilities and interests? Similarly, what should I include to allow low achievers to improve their work? The more flexible you can make these opportunities, the more you will be able to individualize your instruction.

The third prong will doubtless be the most demanding, and probably the scariest. It is to plan for a classroom in which different sorts of activities will be going on at the same time. You might start by arranging for three different sorts of activities: (1) a small number of students being taught together; (2) a section of the class engaged in a cooperative learning activity; and (3) individual stations where students work on individual projects (including enrichment and remedial activities for high and low achievers, as well as projects designed to allow the "kids in the middle" to exhibit their special talents). You could use learning centers for the second and third activities. Both cooperative and individual activities can be conducted in such learning centers. As you think about these options, also consider requesting some assistance from parents, aides, or mentors.

These suggestions reflect only general guidelines. Putting them all together will require a great deal of planning and much flexibility. If you don't mind my saying so, Lisa, I believe you can do it, because you are the sort of teacher who plans carefully but is also able to roll with the punches. I think you could take these guidelines and translate them into specific lesson and unit plans.

I suggest you approach your principal and inquire whether or not you could get some grant money to engage in planning activity and to attend a summer session on individualizing instruction. You could put together a proposal for such a multifunctional classroom, experiment for a year, and write a report or perhaps an article or two on your experience. Such a project would contribute to our understanding of the craft of Christian teaching.

But don't worry too much about your 30—you still have this year to finish. At this time of the year we need to muster additional strength to make it through the doldrums. Pray a lot. Don't let go of the conviction that every single child in your classroom is a precious, gifted image-bearer of God.

Dad

16

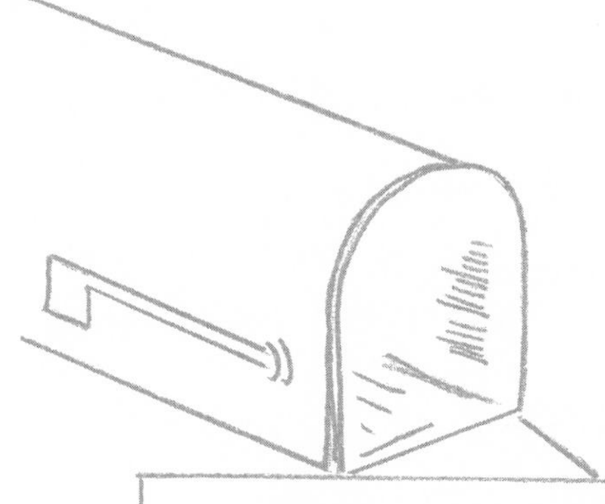

When are students at risk in my classroom?

Subject: "At-risk" inservice
From: Lisa
To: Dad
Date: Fri, 9 Feb 16:25:20 -0600 (CST)

Hi Dad,

Today our staff gathered for an inservice on how to handle at-risk students. An at-risk coordinator from a neighboring school detailed a program their school recently implemented—a program complete with at-risk prevention, at-risk curriculum, at-risk counselors, and at-risk exits for transferring at-risk students to less risky environments.

This isolationist strategy doesn't feel right to me. Did you tell me once that you had written an article on this topic? If so, please zip me a copy.

Love, Lisa

Saturday, February 10

Dear Lisa,

Thanks for your e-mail message. I'm glad to see the staff at your school is considering the issue of at-risk students. Yes, you are right, some time ago I did write an editorial about this matter for the February, 1991, issue of *Christian Educators Journal.* I enclose a copy of this article, as you requested.

Dad

—Guest Editorial by JOHN VAN DYK

Johnny at Risk in a Christian Classroom?

Johnny is a third grader. No one knows for sure just how intelligent the boy really is. At times, to the teacher's delight, he sparkles and shines; but then again he seems to tune out, refuse to work, and turn sullen, the picture of an unmotivated child.

More recently his behavior has become increasingly negative and disruptive, even obnoxious. His teacher, with growing exasperation, checked the cumulative file once more. "Johnny needs attention and discipline," his grade two teacher had written. Like his older brother Billy, Johnny is clearly at risk.

Our schools abound with students more or less "at risk." But what precisely does it mean to be "at risk"? How do we identify an at-risk student? What causes students to become at risk? And what should be done about them? These and similar questions are vigorously debated everywhere in the educational world. Expectedly, there is no consensus about the answers. If there is any agreement at all, perhaps it is that an at-risk student can be roughly described as "a student who is likely to fail in school, either because of learning disabilities or because of behavior problems, or both."

At-risk students, once identified and labeled as such, have a nasty habit of staying stuck in this category. Once at risk, always at risk, it seems. True, some at-risk students settle down and eventually merge with the mainstream, that is, with the students who meet the typical expectations of the teacher, of the curriculum, and of the graduation requirements. But, more often than not, at-risk students are expected to remain at risk. In fact, a youngster thought to be at risk not only stays at risk, but is often expected to fail altogether.

Take Johnny, our third grader, for example. Several years earlier his older brother Billy had been judged to be at risk: at risk to fail as a student. Billy was slow, apparently not all that bright, and pushy. People whispered gossipy stories about his family as well. As time went on Billy became such a recalcitrant, belligerent, intolerable character that he was eventually dismissed from school. The teachers and principal, at their wits' end, no longer knew what to do other than to get rid of him. After all, they said, there is the rotten apple, you know. We don't want to spoil the entire basket! But the dismissal of his brother Billy now confronts Johnny with tremendous odds: his teachers expect him to be like Billy! Though they might not say so, in reality they expect Johnny to fail. Unfortunately for Johnny, such expectations tend to become self-fulfilling prophecies.

At-risk students, especially the behavioral kind, receive plenty of attention and discipline. They are often separated from the main group in order to be tracked into remedial classes or even separate institutions. Some of them, like brother Billy, become intimately acquainted with the principal's office and eventually end up out in the street. Well-intentioned though such attention may be, studies show that these procedures often miss the real problem. While there may be many complicated, even mysterious, reasons for a student to be at risk, often the most fundamental factor is overlooked: a profound sense of alienation, inadequacy, and rejection.

This brings us to consider the Christian classroom once again. Sadly, alienation and rejection are not problems confined to inner-city public schools; they are common experiences in us. When our classrooms are essentially collections of individuals who compete with one another for grades and approval and are taught to be responsible only to themselves and to the teacher, then alienation, rejection, and inadequacy are inevitable consequences, and an at-risk atmosphere will prevail. Students are put at risk because the entire classroom is at risk! When, in addition, teachers engage in mostly whole-group instruction, and ignore or are blind to the individual needs and learning styles of students, the potential for risk is likely to flourish.

Let's look at learning styles, for example. Kenneth and Rita Dunn have shown that something as simple as moving a youngster to a brighter location in the classroom, or replacing incandescent lamps with fluorescent light, has successfully delivered students from the "learning disabled" category. Over and over it has been shown that some students cannot process instructions or information instantaneously and need time to respond. Requiring such students to "pay attention right now!" or subjecting them to time tests puts them at risk. Still other students are simply not able to tune in to the analytic teaching styles so prevalent in junior high and secondary schools. Although such students have all sorts of gifts and abilities, they are not provided with opportunities to shine in their strong areas, and so they, too, are quickly put at risk.

Increasingly, studies show that a collaborative classroom with a warm, accepting, and positive atmosphere is one of the keys to reducing, perhaps even eliminating, the at-risk problem. Cooperative learning strategies, for example, when implemented in a classroom in which the development of trust, shared responsibility, and mutual concern and encouragement are high on the agenda, have been remarkably effective in aiding even those who would otherwise be shunted off as learning disabled or would end up as failures.

In some ways a Christian classroom and an at-risk student constitute a contradiction. True, some of our children are so physically, socially, or emotionally disabled that at-risk seems only their natural condition. And indeed, such children will surely be at risk. Yet, while I recognize the complexity and mystery surrounding the risk, I make bold to claim that even in very severe cases the Christian classroom should be able to accept these children and bring them to experience success according to their gifts. If we teachers could construct a genuinely collaborative classroom, such as I have earlier described in this journal (*CEJ*, December 1989), then the at-risk problem might well be sharply diminished.

Could it be that sometimes the teacher and not the student is really at risk? When Johnny's teacher expects him to fail because his brother Billy failed several years earlier, then is the teacher not putting Johnny at grave risk? If Billy failed, so goes the expectation, then more than likely Johnny will fail, too. Again, when a teacher, often unintentionally, inhibits or ignores the low achievers and favors the high achiever—as Good and Brophy's studies have shown teachers consistently to do (cf. T.L. Good and J.E. Brophy, *Looking in Classrooms*, 1987)—then surely it is primarily the teacher who is at risk, at risk of putting the students at risk.

What is needed is not first of all special remedial programs designed to get the at-risk students on track. After all, being "on track"—often translated to mean "quiet, compliant, and passive"—may conceal or reflect a much more profound at-risk problem than that indicated by the behavior of the "troublemakers." Needed above all, it seems to me, is staff development of the right kind.

Don't get me wrong. I am not out to criticize teachers. I see too many of them who do, in fact, effectively—and often quietly and unnoticed—reduce the at-risk problem in their classrooms. I do believe, however, that all of us teachers need to grow in awareness of what we are doing in the classroom, to grow as reflective practitioners. We teachers need to be increasingly trained to be alert to uniqueness, to the diversity of learning styles, to ways of creating classroom conditions attuned to such variety, and especially to ways of constructing collaborative, caring, accepting, and inviting classrooms.

Such staff development requires visionary principals who can forge their faculty into a team. It requires commitment to build a caring, authentically Christian community, classrooms in which we celebrate gifts rather than assess achievement. It requires a growing sense and practice of collegiality among us teachers. More and more we must open up our classrooms to each other; evaluate and encourage each other's work; freely discuss our strengths, weaknesses, successes, and failures; suggest to one another various ways to improve our teaching effectiveness and our classroom atmosphere; and stay abreast with instructional innovation. Such staff development can surely help us build the kind of classrooms and the kind of schools where the at-risk student will either be a rare exception or only a vague memory.

JVD

John Van Dyk is professor of education and director of the Center for Educational Services at Dordt College in Sioux Center, Iowa.

FEBRUARY 1991 **Christian Educators Journal**
Reprinted with permission.

17

What are some key questions about curriculum?

Subject: Curriculum committee
From: Lisa
To: Dad
Date: Mon, 4 Mar 15:44:27 -0800 (PST)

Hi Dad,

Well, it looks as if the principal thinks I don't have enough to do. He appointed me to a special curriculum study committee. To be honest, Dad, I'm not very excited about such a job. I think it will be a drag, if not a mere formality. I bet my appointment is merely another cog in a creaky wheel grinding out curriculum reports every five years or so—while nothing significant really changes. Just another bureaucratic ho-hum assignment.

On the other hand, I might be able to contribute to the committee's work, and maybe even to the welfare of the entire school! I know what you will say. Go for it! Don't say no to a challenge with the potential of making a major impact. Right? Well, I already shuffled through my old college texts to see if I could find something about curriculum. My committee assignment also mentioned something about a *Christian* approach to curriculum. That mandate will make the job even more demanding.

The committee includes several colleagues and a member or two from the education committee. Our mandate is to review the language arts and math curriculum from Kindergarten through sixth grade. That's just about half the entire curriculum right there! And frankly, Dad, I'm worried about the composition of the committee. A couple of the teachers on it are people with whom I have had some pesky differences of opinion in the past.

I know you're more into instructional than curricular matters, Dad. Nevertheless, maybe you have some ideas to get started.

Love, Lisa

Subject: Re: Curriculum committee
From: Dad
To: Lisa
Date: Mon, 4 Mar 22:06:14 -0600 (CST)

Dear Lisa,

Congratulations! Yes, you guessed correctly: I advise you to go for it! I think you can do some very significant things as a member of this study committee. Of course, from where I sit I cannot advise you very well, especially since I do not know the ins and outs of the curriculum currently in place in your school. Maybe it is such a fantastic curriculum that you should not tamper with it at all! You have heard the old cliché: if it ain't broke, don't try to fix it!

However, usually there is room for review. After all, times change, resources change, students change, and expectations change. No doubt taking another look at this curriculum is not a waste of time. But how to approach the job, you ask?

I suggest that as soon as your committee gets together to tackle the project, you raise three important questions: First, how important to the committee members is the theme of "Christian perspective"? You know what I mean: often our main concern is the stuff that makes up our curriculum, and not so much the philosophy that undergirds it. Christian perspective can be treated as an assumption to be passed over. After all, your school has an eloquent mission statement, and most of you can say something significant and impressive about your goals as Christian teachers. Nevertheless, I encourage you to bring the issue up front: Is there institutional—and committee—commitment to the importance of Christian perspective in curriculum? How strong is this commitment? Is it strong enough to allow you, as a team, to ask some very hard questions about the whys and wherefores of your forthcoming committee recommendations?

Here is the second question to be posed before you begin your work: What concept of curriculum are we working with? For the purposes of our work as a committee, what does the term "curriculum" encompass? You see, your definition of curriculum will strongly influence your discussion and conclusions.

For example, if your committee believes that curriculum is basically a *program of studies*, to be outlined in a curriculum guide, then you will be handicapped at the outset. If curriculum is essentially a matter of *content* to be arranged and sequenced, then of course your committee will do little more than shuffle around various chunks of subject matter. You will be asking questions like, When should our children learn about Australian salamanders, in grade 3 or 4?

Don't settle for such a narrow definition, Lisa. Push for a larger, dynamic concept of curriculum, one which not only deals with content, scope, and sequence but also with questions of goals, teaching approaches, and student learning. Avoid perennialist and essentialist reductions that see the curriculum as some kind of static road map. A definition of curriculum I like goes something like this: curriculum is a dynamic, organized plan for teaching and learning. Every word in this definition is important: curriculum is a plan, so we need to select content and skills. It is organized, so we have to consider scope and sequence. It is dynamic: it is ever-changing because classroom situations change, children are diverse learners, and our changing world makes changing demands. The little word "for" points to goals and direction. And, equally important, a curriculum plan needs to suggest teaching approaches and recognize student levels of development, readiness, and learning styles.

Finally, one more question you should put to the committee. It picks up on what I just said about the little word "for": What is the *overarching* goal of the curriculum you are going to review and revise? What is the ultimate outcome? If you do not insist on an answer to this question, your committee may come up with recommendations that go in a dozen different directions. The overarching goal of your school should provide the framework and direction for your work.

What should this goal be? You and I have discussed it before: to equip our students "for works of service," as the Apostle Paul puts it in Ephesians 4:11-12, to prepare them for knowledgeable and competent discipleship. To be a disciple of the Lord, one who functions effectively as a Christian in a broken and hurting world, requires a lot of knowledge and a lot of competence. To prepare children for this task will require continuous reflection on what and how we teach. This is not just a matter of shuffling a bit of content around.

You mentioned that you looked through some of your old college textbooks on curriculum. Have you looked at Harro Van Brummelen's book *Stepping Stones to a Christian Curriculum*? It can serve you well. If I were you, I would recommend that every member of the committee study this book, and that you discuss it as a group.

I understand you will attend your first meeting in a week or so. Let me know what you think of these three questions, and please keep me posted on the progress that I know you will make.

As always, Dad

18

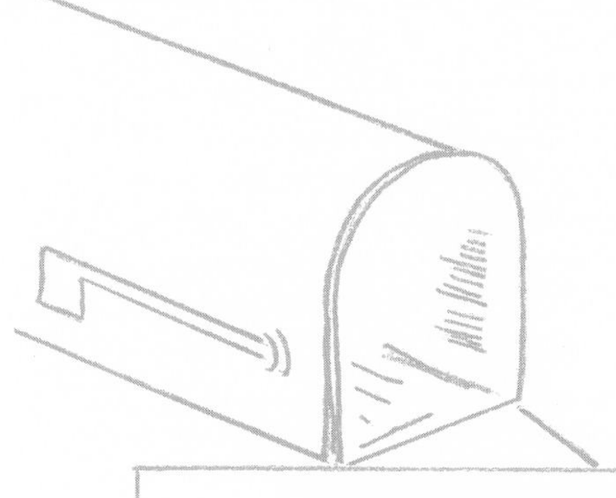

What is a Christian perspective on curriculum?

Subject: Curriculum committee again!
From: Lisa
To: Dad
Date: Mon, 18 Mar 16:36:44 -0800 (PST)

Hi Dad,

At first I thought I should call you, but then I decided to send a quick e-mail message instead. I just got out of the second curriculum committee meeting, and, frankly, I'm about to tear my hair out! I know I sound terribly judgmental again, but the fact is that some of the committee members are getting on my nerves. At the first meeting I proposed the questions you suggested in your last letter to me. I asked how committed we really are to search for a *Christian* perspective on curriculum, what *concept* of curriculum we are working with, and for what overarching goal we should aim. Although there was some encouraging support, there was plenty of cold-shouldered skepticism. I was particularly disturbed by my colleagues' insinuations that my questions imply a lack of commitment on their part, or even a weak faith. "How do you dare ask," they demanded, "whether or not a Christian perspective on curriculum is important to us? After all, aren't we all devoted Christians?"

Now isn't this wild? *Of course* I'm not questioning anybody's faith. You know, Dad, it's weird how defensive we become when we are asked to assess our commitment to Christian education. Why do you suppose we react this way? Anyway, I know that you will urge me to keep asking the tough questions. My question to you, Dad, is, How can we be sure our committee's *curriculum proposals* reflect a Christian perspective? Some thoughts on this point will be welcome—no need to lecture me about how to get along with my colleagues, okay?

Love, Lisa

Monday evening, March 18

Dear Lisa,

Okay, no lectures on winning friends and influencing colleagues! Let me answer some of your questions. First, there is this defensiveness about our commitments. Maybe it is the doctrine of perseverance of the saints—once a Christian, always a Christian: no need to discuss the status of our commitment. We exempt ourselves from asking tough questions about how our Christian faith comes to expression especially in matters of curriculum and teaching. Somehow we have come to believe that a Christian teacher and a roomful of children of Christian parents produce instant Christian education; consequently, questions about what makes a curriculum Christian or about how to teach Christianly can be summarily dismissed. I suspect that these assumptions lie behind the cool reception you received.

But now to the more significant issue: How can your committee's revised curriculum proposals reflect a Christian perspective? Let me suggest a few more guidelines to toss into the hopper.

Consider the central story of the Bible: the creation of the world, the fall into sin, and the ongoing redemption through the sacrifice of Jesus Christ. This story, it seems to me, should be built right into the very heart of the subject matter we teach. After all, is there any part of the curriculum you teach that somehow is not part of created reality, as the philosophers put it? The entire universe is created by God, designed by God, and is moment-by-moment upheld by God, through the power of Jesus Christ. A Christian school curriculum will have to make this theme very clear. You might suggest a bit of Bible study here. For example, look at Genesis 1, Psalms 33 and 145, John 1:1, and Hebrews 1:3. I know, all of this sounds like a lot of heavy theology. Yet, apart from this broad perspective, what point is there to teaching our subject matter?

But equally clear will have to be the dark picture of the fall into sin, a disaster which affected everything, nothing excluded.

Throughout the entire curriculum, our children must see the awful, deforming consequences of sin. They must recognize the right (God's intent for the world) and the wrong (the sinful distortions) in every corner of culture, in all the manifold dimensions of human life. But we must not leave our children staring at sin. The redemption of Christ—who died to reconcile *all things* to God the Father, as we read in Colossians 1—promises hope and gives us a vision of the Kingdom of God, a Kingdom here already now and to be fully completed in times to come. So our curriculum must show our children the way of reconciliation, healing, and justice. It must point them to evidences of the shalom that will be fully here when Christ returns.

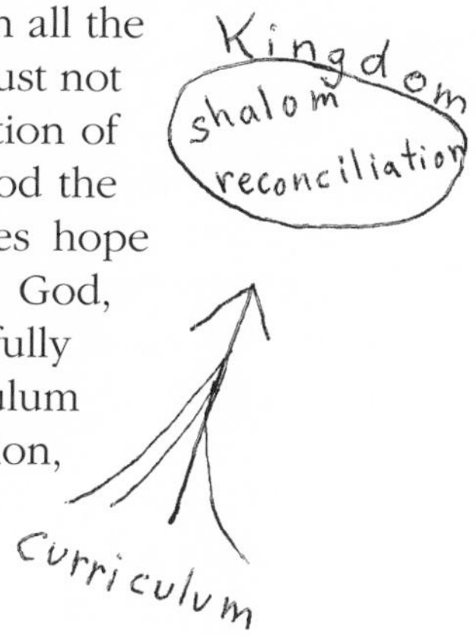

So you see, Lisa, a curriculum which teaches only factual knowledge and marketable skills is not really a *Christian* curriculum. Such a curriculum might be proposed by some state education departments, but it falls far short of what Christian teaching is all about.

My reference to factual knowledge and marketable skills suggests a second guideline: What concept of knowledge is your curriculum committee working with? Currently there is much discussion about not only what knowledge is worth teaching but also what knowledge really is in the first place. We shall have to talk more about this some time. Meanwhile, the Bible gives us some important insight into the nature of knowledge. Sit down sometime, take a good concordance, and check out some of the key passages. I think, for example, of Psalm 111: "[A] good understanding have all they who *do* his commandments." This verse tells us that knowledge without action is not really knowledge at all. I may be a quiz show whiz and know all the facts listed in the *Encyclopedia Britannica*, but if I don't *do* something with these facts, if I do not bring them into a life of service, my supposed knowledge is empty wizardry. Or think of Paul's statement in I Corinthians 13: "If I have all the knowledge in the world"—and that's quite a bit, nowadays!—"but have not love, I am nothing." What is Paul saying here? Well, for one thing, he rejects the idea that knowledge is essentially academic, intellectual stuff and nothing more. I can be an expert in my field and fathom the profoundest theories about the universe, but without love my expertise is empty fluff.

A Biblical view of knowledge, in other words, involves the *whole* person, not just the brain. You should press this point in your committee, Lisa. Frequently pose this question: How will the content, skills, and teaching strategies you select contribute to the development of the *whole* child, not just make him smarter in math and grammar or some other subject? How will the curriculum help deepen the commitment of our children to the Lord? How will it equip for service?

Related to this second guideline is a third: it has to do with the view of the (whole) child the curriculum assumes. For example, if we believe that students are essentially empty-headed dunderheads, our curriculum will probably stress heaps of information to be stored in the brain. Our aim will be to deposit a mass of facts into the containers the students presumably carry around on their shoulders.

If, on the other hand, we assume that children are gifted with all kinds of abilities and come into a classroom with a wealth of experience, we will design an altogether different curriculum, one that will probably stress the development of thinking skills, responsibility, and preparation for life-long learning.

So what does this challenge mean for your committee? Clearly, the view of youngsters as empty-headed dunderheads must be rejected. Such a view denigrates the image of God in each one of our children. The second view seems to do more justice to the giftedness of our students. But it does not go far enough. We need to recognize the multifaceted natures of our children. A Christian curriculum, therefore, will attach importance to what are often regarded as frills. Art and music, for example, should be regarded as *basics,* not a dispensable luxury relegated to an occasional last class period in the day. And physical training and health education will be viewed as vitally important in our sedentary age.

So what, in sum, are the guidelines I suggest? First, the entire curriculum should reflect the great biblical themes of creation, the fall into sin, and the cosmic redemption in Christ. Second, be sure you work with a biblical concept of knowledge. True knowledge leads to committed action. And third, avoid a narrow focus on academic stuff, but aim to make the curriculum address the multifaceted nature of our children.

Well, I hope that these guidelines will give your committee something to think about and talk about. No doubt you will run into more frustrations. Try not to let it ruffle you. Remember, kindness and patience are important fruits of the Spirit. So, yes, press hard, but at the same time, do so in love and with gentleness. Oops—I'm lecturing you after all!

Do keep me posted on how things are going.

Dad

19

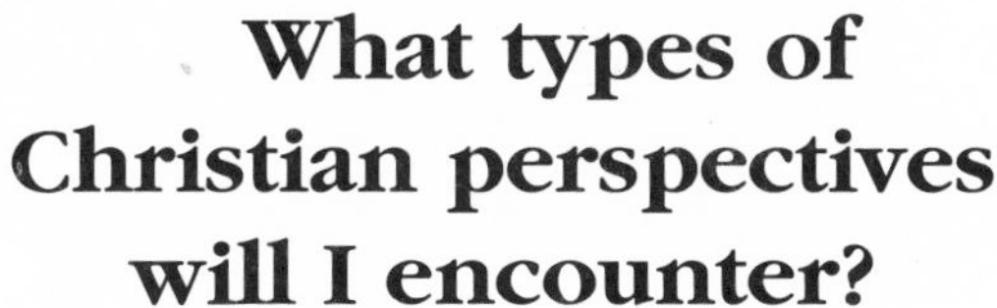

What types of Christian perspectives will I encounter?

```
Subject: Christian perspectives
From: Dad
To: Lisa
Date: Mon, 25 Mar  09:22:14 -0600 (CST)
```

Hi Dad,

Hallelujah! We're done—at least with our preliminary curriculum report. It's quite an accomplishment considering all the arguments within the committee. I thought that once we all committed ourselves to integrating a Christian perspective, the ride would be downhill. It wasn't, and I'm still not sure why. Anyway, I sent you our report by snail-mail. Only you would read an educational report for fun!

Love, Lisa

Tuesday, April 2

Dear Lisa,

Thank you very much for the copy of the preliminary report your curriculum committee put together. I assume that it has been distributed to the staff and board members for further comment and input. I see you folks have gone well beyond a listing of subject matter and skills to be taught at specific levels. Clearly the committee avoided a mere content-shuffling exercise. Great! I know you have experienced some frustration; nevertheless, I commend you for steadfastly pressing the issue of perspective.

The question of perspective, of course, is of fundamental importance to the life of a school. As has been said so often—so pardon me for saying it once more—perspective determines, consciously or unconsciously, what you do in the classroom, what your colleagues do, and what your principal does. So I am always glad when I see Christian schools taking the issue of perspective seriously.

Articulating and implementing perspective often leads to disagreement and conflict. One reason for this is that education is a complicated affair. It's so easy to generalize about perspective, but as soon as we ask questions about nitty-gritty specifics, differences of opinion emerge. Another reason is that we do not always recognize that there can be different Christian perspectives operating within the framework of a single school.

I can identify at least three different types of Christian perspective. The first of these is well-known to you, and to most of us: in fact, volumes have been written about it. It is the perspective we usually designate as *dualism*. Dualism proposes that what distinguishes a Christian school from a public school is the presence of (1) Bible study, (2) devotional exercises such as prayer and chapel, and (3) a stress on explicitly Christian moral behavior. At the same time, the curriculum and teaching methods do not differ much, if at all, from what you would find in a public school. After all, math is math and Spanish is Spanish—these subjects presumably have little or nothing to do with the Christian faith.

A dualistic school usually exudes a distinct Christian atmosphere. You walk in and you see Bible texts all over the place and the students are well-behaved. There is singing and prayer. Discipline is swift and consistent. No wonder that parents are willing to pay large sums of money to have their children educated in such a controlled environment.

My critique of dualism is not that it is unchristian. Of course not. The problem is that dualism is incomplete—it is reductionistic, we might say. It does not go far enough. It limits the Lordship of Christ: Jesus is Lord of our personal lives, but has little or nothing to say about the content of the curriculum.

A second perspective we might dub "tacky." By "tacky" I mean that this approach "tacks on" Christian language to an educational practice that remains essentially untouched by the Gospel. For example, in grammar we might ask the children to diagram sentences from the Bible. In math we say something about God's design and leave it at that. In science we acknowledge that God created it all and from then on nothing specifically Christian is heard.

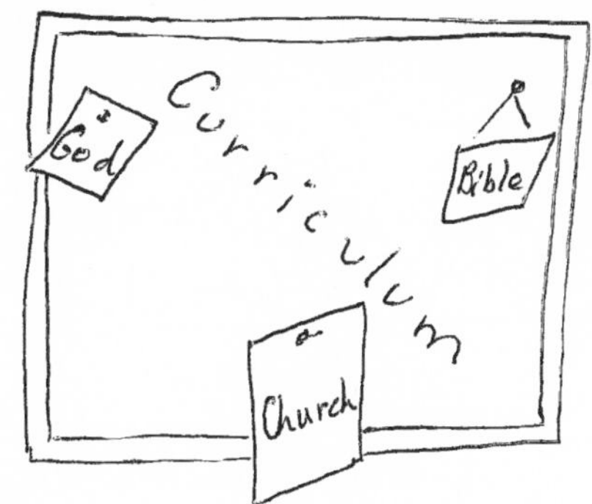

You recognize, Lisa, that "tackiness" is similar to dualism. The difference is that while dualism explicitly, in an up-front fashion, acknowledges that curriculum is a separate area independent of the Gospel, a tacky approach seeks to give the *appearance* of a thoroughly integrated Christian perspective by scattering and sprinkling "God words" through the curriculum. There are, in fact, curriculums on the market that try to make themselves *look* Christian by adding Bible texts here or there, or little phrases such as "at the end of your math lesson, thank Jesus for giving you patience and determination," or some such thing.

A tacky approach is a misleading approach. It fools you into believing that we have an authentic Christian perspective when in fact it merely hides an essentially secular curriculum. I see some of my curriculum students fall for this sort of thing. I ask them to examine a variety of curriculum materials and write some reactions. Invariably some of the students will be deeply impressed by a curriculum that tacks on a lot of Bible texts and "God talk."

Other students, however, will see through the fluff and recognize that dualistic and tacky approaches are problematic. Instead, we need to encourage a third approach, namely an *authentically* Christian approach. This is the approach I tried to outline for you in my previous two letters. This approach intentionally aims to place *all* our educational work, the *entire* curriculum, our teaching strategies, our classroom management, and even the way we organize our classroom in a Christian, biblical perspective.

But now I must sound an important warning: Sometimes, Lisa, an authentic perspective can still be reductionistic. You say: "How can this be? Doesn't 'authentic' mean just that? Genuine and complete?" Well, yes, in a way. My concern is that sometimes teachers in Christian schools believe that their task is finished when the students have acquired a Christian perspective on specific subject matter. I am concerned about what we may call "perspectivalism"—the idea that when our students have learned to understand and articulate a Christian perspective, we need do nothing more.

What is missing? I'll go back to a comment I made in an earlier letter to you. Knowledge is knowledge only if it leads to concrete action. Perspective—no matter how authentic—is authentic perspective only if it leads to action. Perspective is not enough by itself. It must be translated into active, responsible discipleship.

So I worry that we *talk* a lot of perspective but do not always *practice* perspective. Needed are classroom situations which allow students to practice the perspective they learn. Often this application will involve service projects. You have heard about the Christian school whose biology class cleaned up the polluted creek that flowed by the campus. Often such projects lead to off-campus activities. A social studies class, for example, may visit a Native American reservation and design ways of providing assistance. An English class may lead to writing letters or reading novels to shut-ins. Joan Stob, in her book *Educating for Responsible Service,* provides a legion of examples.

The point here is that perspectivalism works with an unexamined assumption: that merely *exposing* students to insight will lead to changed lives and action. But this is a false assumption, as you and I well know. Most of us *know* what is right, yet do not always *do* what is right. Sometimes we don't do what is right because of our perverse, sinful nature. At other times we don't do it simply because we don't know *how* to do it—we have never really been taught and we have never had opportunity to practice. For example, we Christians often get embroiled in needless controversy simply because we have not learned appropriate procedures for conflict resolution.

I suggest that you and your colleagues commit yourselves to a continuous reexamination of the curriculum. Perhaps every one of the teachers should be asked: How can my students take the material learned in my class and translate it into responsible action? To answer this question you will need the insights and the input of the students themselves. They themselves will have to come up with ways in which their learning can affect their lives, now and in the future.

I am encouraged by your curriculum committee's report, Lisa. It looks to me that it strives to avoid on the one hand both dualism and tacky views of subject matter and skills, and perspectivalism on the other. What a challenge it is to describe and implement an authentic Christian perspective. It can't be done without much prayer and the support of the Holy Spirit.

You folks are on the right track, Lisa! Don't let up now!

Dad

20

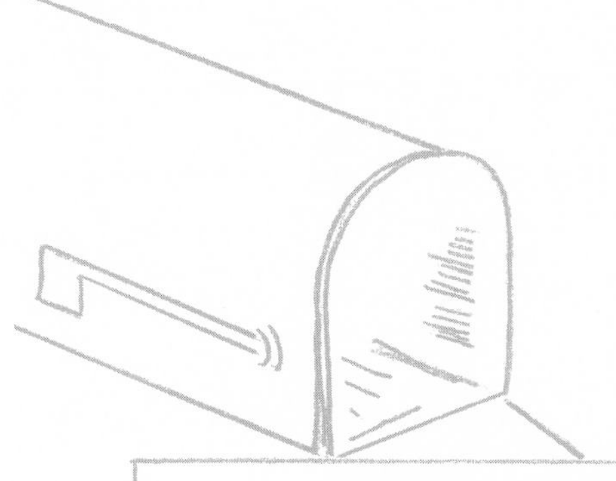

Can a Christian teach Christianly in a public school?

Apr. 6

Hi Dad,

I'm on spring break. Nice to get out of town for a bit. I had a delightful coffee date with my old roommate Vonda. She teaches fifth grade in the public school here. Had quite a discussion about Christians teaching in public schools. What do you think, Dad—Is it possible to teach Christianly in a public school?

I plan to be back in my classroom by the middle of next week.

Love,

Lisa

Wednesday, April 10

Dear Lisa,

I was happy to hear about last Saturday's coffee date with Vonda. I take it you enjoyed your customary banana cream pie, as well as the discussion about the question of Christians teaching in public schools. Some suggest that Christian teachers should not take jobs in public schools, any more than that conservative Baptists can participate in Mormon tabernacle worship services. On the other extreme are those who argue that all Christian teachers should get into public schools. If we were to close the Christian schools, they say, and use all of our teaching talents in the public school, what a difference we could make! And the tuition money we would save could be used to help the starving and the poor.

Well, should Christians teach in a public school? Your friend has obviously said yes. But did you ask her how it feels to teach in a public school, to be prevented by law from talking about the Lord? You tell me that she, like you, teaches a self-contained fifth-grade class. Did you ask her how she can truthfully teach science without the opportunity of displaying God's marvelous hand in it all? And how can she teach social studies without reference to God's laws for family, marriage, and government?

Questions like these are commonly posed by fans of Christian schools. But I say, slow down a bit! Put on some brakes here! Before we bubble over with critical remarks about the handicaps Christian teachers face in public schools, let's ask another pertinent, though at first sight unusual question: Can Christian teachers really teach Christianly in a Christian school? Now before you start chuckling at this seemingly absurd question, let me remind you that I have been in Christian schools where I seriously doubt genuine Christian teaching is possible.

Of course, it depends on what you mean by "teaching Christianly." If you mean opening the school day with a prayer and some devotions and sprinkling about a few Bible texts here and there, then yes, teaching Christianly is possible only in a Christian school and not in a public school. But if you mean what I mean, namely, the kind of teaching that guides students towards knowledgeable and competent discipleship, well, then I have more than one concern.

For one thing, I think of the structure of our Christian schools. In many ways they are identical to public schools, and in some ways they have not changed in a hundred years. I mean such things as short class periods, bells ringing, children mass taught while sitting in rows, teachers talking for more than 85% of the time, grading, sorting, competition, and on and on. What kind of discipleship can we really teach in such an environment?

Or look at the curriculum. You will find many a Christian school curriculum chopped up and fragmented into unrelated pieces. Talking about God here and there is not going to prevent our children from catching a fractured picture of what should be understood as a beautiful, coherent, interrelated creation. Think also about the appalling lack of community in numerous Christian schools, when teaching Christianly should mean, among other things, inducting our children into a real community. But what do we see? Individual teachers cooped up in their classrooms with hardly a moment to confer with a colleague, infighting and strife, contradictory philosophies, conflict between principal and staff or board. Moreover, some parents give only lip service to the talk about Christian discipleship; in actuality such talk is mere "warm fuzzies" to them, as in reality they look for the schools to teach their children to be ambitious, success-seeking individuals, trained in the American way of consumerism.

Can you teach Christianly in a Christian school? Can you really teach the children to become radical, self-effacing disciples of the Lord, Christians who will be out to sacrifice themselves for the poor, the widow, and the orphan? Are we exiting graduates who, in fact, prophetically address the sinfulness of much of our cozy, comfortable, more-is-better style of life? Could you teach these values without running into serious trouble with the school authorities and parents?

Thank the Lord that there are Christian schools where such teaching is possible and even encouraged. How long such schools will survive is another question. But that is not my point. My point is that our critique of public schools should not smugly assume that all is well in our Christian schools.

As you know, Lisa, I do believe that Christians can teach in public schools, and that some should. It is fundamentally a matter of calling. Of course, one thing remains non-negotiable: Wherever we teach, we must teach Christianly—no matter what the constraints. We have no choice but to be *Christian* teachers.

If you feel called to teach, in other words, you had better commit yourself to teach Christianly. But can we do that in a public school? Even if we concede that many a Christian school, too, stifles true Christian teaching, is it not the case that in a public school the legal constraints are overwhelming?

Here one must make a personal choice, it seems to me. If you are the kind of person who bubbles over with love for the Lord, and on whose lips are unending hallelujahs, then maybe you should reconsider accepting a position in a public school. Such hallelujahs will eventually offend some parents who have no sympathy for the Christian religion. You and I would soon be offended if the teacher of our child in the public school bubbled over with enthusiasm for same-sex marriage or New Age philosophy. In other words, if you cannot be low-key and subtle about your love for the Lord, don't teach in a public school.

But if you can communicate without explicit religious language, then, of course, public school classrooms still offer splendid opportunities for guiding and modeling. You can display the joy, comfort, and stability of resting in the Lord. Your entire demeanor can point in a redemptive direction. When it comes to unfolding subject matter, however, you will immediately feel the legal constraints. You can, of course, decide that you will spread the Gospel anyway, but then do realize that you are breaking the law, and if this should culminate in your dismissal, then so be it.

Nevertheless, I would encourage the Christian public school teacher to look for subject matter that allows the students to grasp something of discipleship without proselytizing. For example, you might explore integration of subject matter, and stress how knowledge should lead to right action. Ask questions that prompt students to examine their assumptions and beliefs. Seek to show that every view of life is based on faith of one kind or another.

Over the last few years I have conducted numerous summer sessions for teachers who left the public schools in order to teach in Christian schools. Their complaint has a universal ring: "I just feel I really cannot teach Christianly in a public school!" But then, there also are teachers who dropped out of Christian schools on the same grounds. Their idealism and enthusiasm were completely destroyed by the strait-jacketing, conformity-promoting structures they experienced in Christian schools. Their vision of teaching Christianly, of equipping students for discipleship, simply had no chance of being realized in the Christian school. So they left, disillusioned and disenchanted.

So I urge you, Lisa, to recognize the complexity of the question. Deciding on teaching Christianly in a public or Christian school is not just a simple yes or no affair. Take into account the nature of the schools, their structures, their goals, their supporting communities, and the sorts of students they seek to serve.

I assume that you will have another coffee and pie date with your friend some day. Maybe at that time you can begin to unravel these issues further.

Dad

21

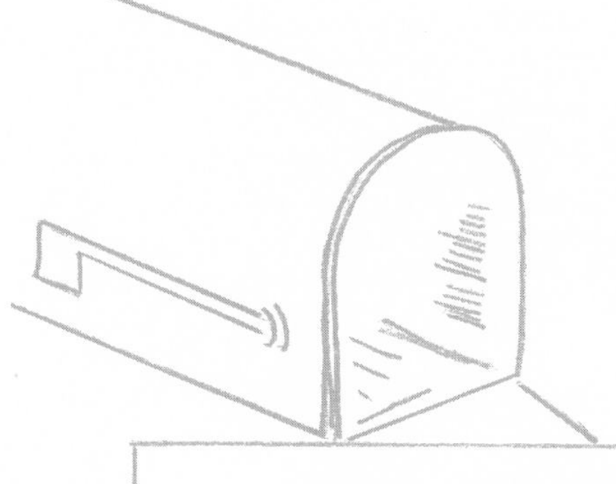

How important are classroom devotions?

Apr. 25

Hi Dad,

A long time ago you said something about devotions in the classroom. You know something? I think my classroom devotions are getting to be pretty stale—so stale, in fact, that I think that sometimes I could just as easily omit them. But then I would run into trouble with parents, I'm sure. Some of them are still dualistic—as you would call it—thinking that devotions are what makes the school really Christian. I should tell you that I'm not the only teacher who complains about devotions. Can you recall for me what you once told me about this problem? Or maybe you have some fresh ideas?

Love,
Lisa

Thursday, May 2

Dear Lisa,

Your recent letter voices a common complaint. Classroom devotional activities so often seem flat and pointless, yes, even downright boring—sort of ho-hum at best. They easily degenerate into a stifling routine. The students expect devotions but don't expect anything *from* them. Even though we try to get the children involved—by prayer requests, for example—it often looks as if devotions don't do much except promise another routine day in the classroom.

Your complaint is not unique, Lisa. When I talk with teachers about devotions, I am frequently asked to suggest resources and activities. Sure, there is plenty of devotional literature on the market. Every Christian bookstore carries stacks of books you can use in the classroom. But the use of such materials quickly gets old. And it often leaves the children passive and only peripherally involved.

You know, there are Christian school teachers—maybe even in your school—who have virtually no interest in doing devotions in class. They believe that devotions belong in the home and in the church—not in the school. After all, school is for academics, they say. I know that you do not share their view. No, devotional activity is not superfluous or misplaced, just as in our personal life we can not postpone devotions until we're in church or gathered around the dinner table.

Others confuse devotions with spirituality. If we equate the two, we will believe that the *Christian* part of the school can be bottled up in a few minutes of Bible reading and prayer, leaving the remainder of the school day untouched by the claims of the Lord. What is the difference between devotions and spiritual activity? The word "spiritual" means "gripped and directed by the Holy Spirit." All of our life, from beginning to end, 24 hours a day, is to be "spiritual"—an arm-in-arm walk with the Holy Spirit (see Gal. 5). To be spiritual is like being married: it's a full-time commitment, an all or nothing kind of thing.

Devotions, on the other hand, are but one form of spiritual activity. Human life comes to expression in a multitude of ways: eating, socializing, studying, teaching, relaxing, worshipping, and having devotions. All of these count as different kinds of spiritual activities. So what is the relationship between spiritual activities and devotions? We can put it as follows: all devotional activities are spiritual activities, but not every spiritual activity is a devotional activity.

Enough philosophy. Ask yourself: What guidelines should govern my classroom devotions? What should my classroom devotions strive to accomplish? And how can I avoid having our devotions turn into traditional and meaningless repetition? Let me suggest some directions.

First of all, devotions should aim to deepen the commitment of all involved. They should bring us closer to God. They should help us experience a special, close relationship between the Lord and ourselves. If they indeed do this, other things will happen too. For example, effective devotional activity will help set the tone for the work to be done the rest of the day. For that reason devotions are often held first thing in the morning. Devotions will be especially helpful if they are *connected* to the day's curriculum. They should tie into and prepare for the day's classroom activities.

Devotions should also involve the *whole* child, not just his brain. If we ask the children to merely *think* about devotional themes, they will probably remain detached.

So we should aim to have our students become emotionally and physically involved. Thinking cannot be eliminated, of course, but perhaps our "devotional thinking" should be of a more meditative and contemplative kind.

Devotions should be a positive and encouraging experience. Even when there are reasons to mourn or to weep together, devotions should help the participants to see a loving God who embraces us and walks with us even when our journey takes us through deep and dark valleys. As a result, devotional activity will promote community in the classroom. Our children will have opportunity to share with each other and care for one another. In small groups they can talk about both ordinary and special gifts the Lord has given them, and together give thanks for them; or they can share their needs and pray for one another. In small groups and whole-class settings the teacher and the children can suggest ways of learning to praise God.

Now I just mentioned the word "learn." One of the big problems, I think, is that we expect the children to know how to engage in devotions. Such expectation is not unreasonable, of course. After all, haven't most of our children been in church and

Sunday school for years already, and didn't their parents teach them to "say their prayers" at bedtime? Think of your own experience, Lisa. Nevertheless, I am convinced that we need to spend more time *preparing* the students for devotions. Just as we need to teach the children the skills required for group work, so we need to help them develop their devotional skills.

We might begin such instruction by spending some time discussing what we can and should *expect* from devotional activities. We need to make sure to solicit ideas from the children. Do we *expect* to meet with God? Do we really *believe* that the Lord will spend time with us, invisibly but nevertheless *real*, right here in our classroom? And what can we expect from each other as we talk with the Lord?

Secondly, we should make an effort to teach the children the sorts of behavior appropriate in devotions. We know, of course, about folding our hands and closing our eyes. And children love to do motions when singing songs or reciting Bible verses. There is no reason why we should not extend these customs to include bending our knees, raising our hands, and bowing our heads low. In addition, it is important that the children know how to relate to one another during devotions. Having them hold hands is surely a good way to start. It is a good idea to have the children *practice* expressing love and concern for each other. Put-downs come naturally. But words of praise and encouragement or of comfort need specific practice and plenty of it. You recall this point from our conversations about cooperative learning.

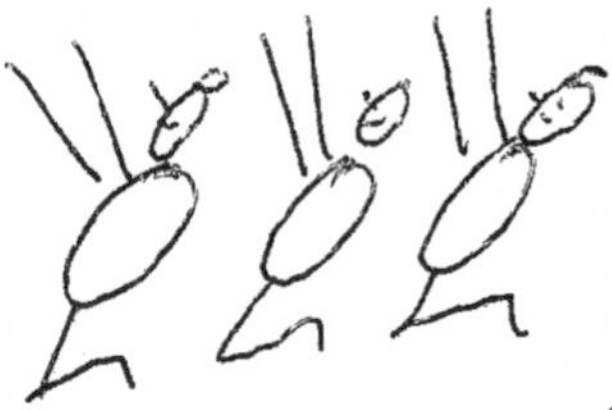

Let's make these guidelines more concrete by describing a few examples of the sort of devotions we need to cultivate. I think of a fourth-grade teacher about to begin a new science unit on the senses. He decided to tie devotions into the unit. So he began devotions by saying: "Imagine that the Lord is deaf and can't hear us. How can we show him that we love him and that we want to love each other? If He can see but not hear, how can we make this clear to Him?" The children brainstormed and came up with suggestions: bend our knees, bow our heads, then lift our arms. Do a dance. Write a big sign saying: "Lord, we love you!" Then take turns embracing each other to show God our brotherly and sisterly love. And so on.

Another teacher introduced a lesson in language arts by asking her students to write a brief meditation, including a prayer, which they then shared in small groups. The teacher modeled this activity by writing and sharing her own meditation. Still another language arts teacher asked her students to write a letter to God.

Finally, Lisa, designing effective devotional activity should be a staff project. It is the sort of thing that flourishes only if we link up with one another and pool our resources, creativity, and experiences. Why not propose to your principal that the board set some money aside for a week-long brainstorming session next summer? Who knows what might come out of such a project: probably a set of wonderful ideas that you could share with teachers in other Christian schools and, of course, with me!

Dad

22

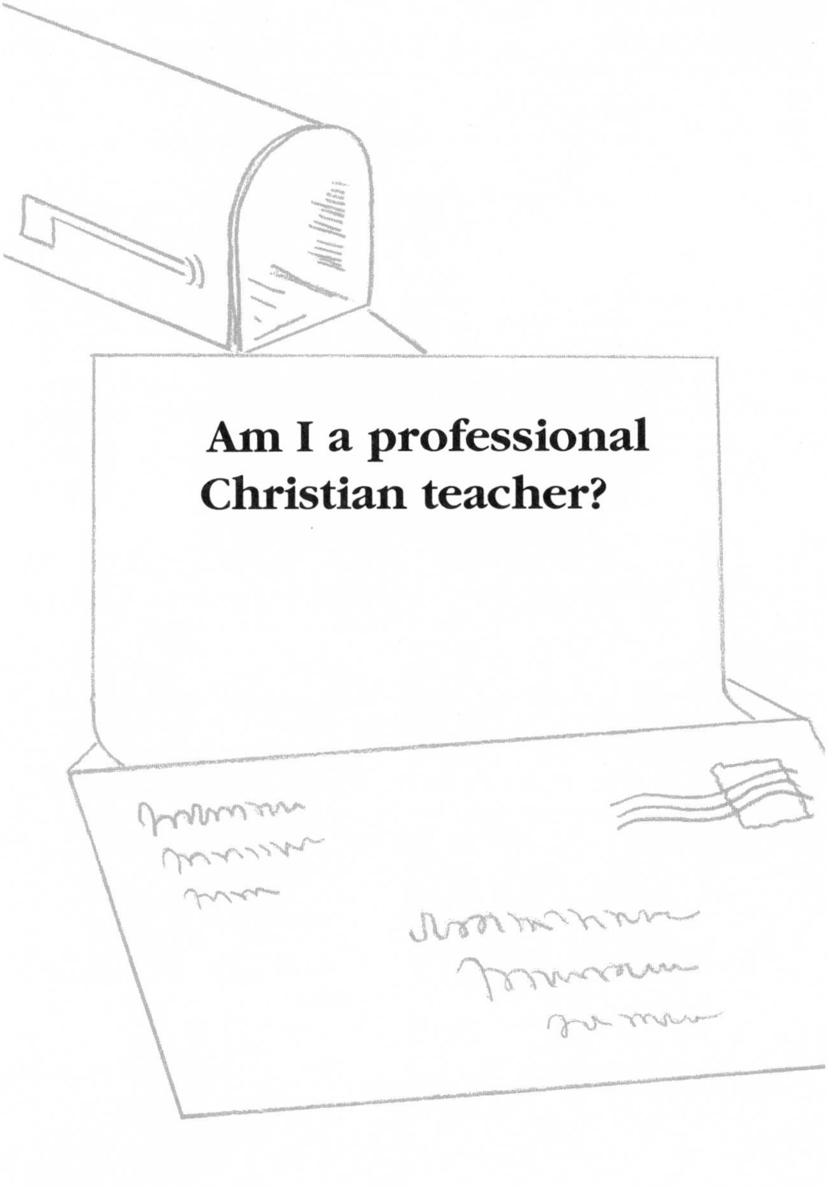

Am I a professional Christian teacher?

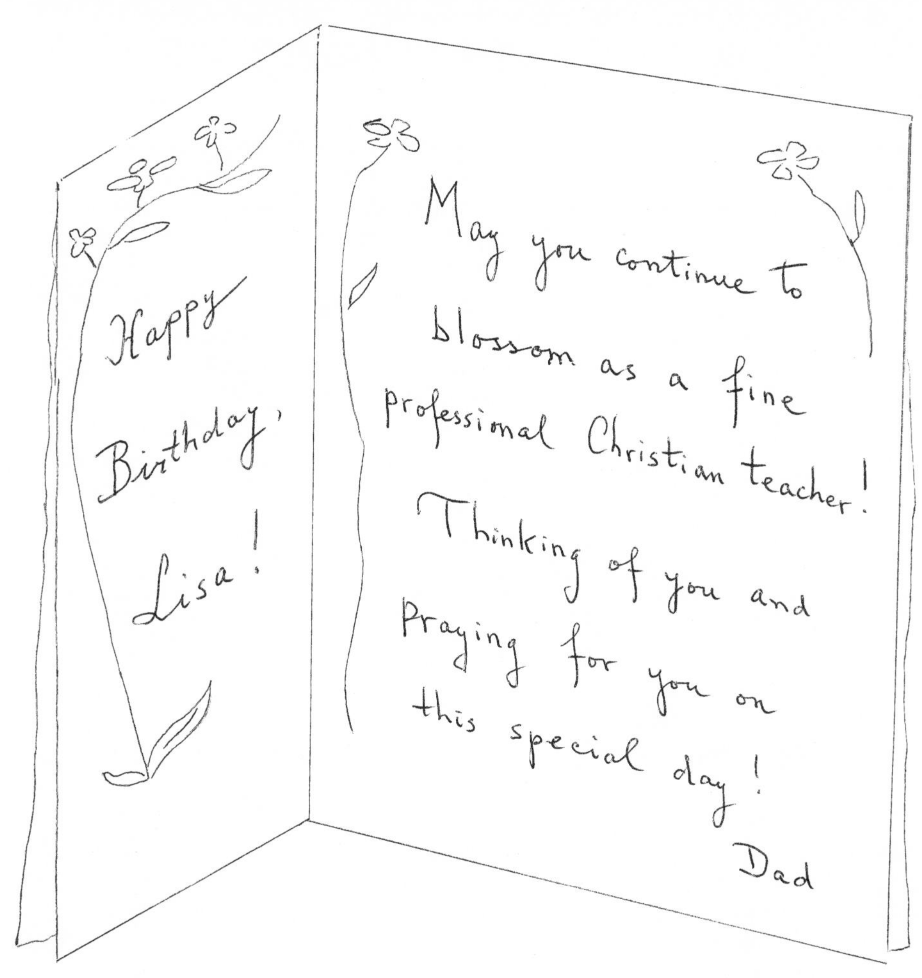

Subject: Birthday card
From: Lisa
To: Dad
Date: Fri, 17 May 16:54:44 -0700 (PDT)

Hi Dad,

I tried to call you, but you were out of town on a speaking engagement. So I'll write a quick e-mail message to say thank-you for the card and birthday wishes. I really love that line, "blossom as a fine professional Christian teacher." Believe me, Dad, I'm trying hard! And guess what: I do think I'm on the way.

Like you, I take my work very seriously. I don't see my teaching task as merely a humdrum job, something to do for pay and long summer vacations. On the contrary, I see my classroom responsibility as a special calling from the Lord. I work in my school as an office bearer, called to do an important task in the Kingdom of God. *Office consciousness* is what you call this, right, Dad? The term may be nothing but jargon to some, but, to be honest, I've actually found the concept of office consciousness helpful—especially when I'm down and blue and wonder whether I really should have become a teacher. You know of such times, too, when it looks as if the job is just too overwhelming. Whenever that happens—sometimes too often!—I do two things: First, I pray. Then I remember that God has called me to the office of teacher. As you have reminded me more than once, the Lord does not call us to a task we can't do. He equips us. I think of the story of Moses, who fussed and complained that he did not have the competence to face Pharaoh. "Lord," he objected, "I have marbles in my mouth!" But the Lord ordered Moses to go anyway. He promised to enable Moses to carry out his assignment in Egypt land. I love that story, Dad. Though I'm sure I do not look like him, Moses is a bit of a role model for me.

Anyway, thanks again for the card.

Love, Lisa

Subject: Re: Birthday card
From: Dad
To: Lisa
Date: Sat, 18 May 10:11:43 -0500 (CDT)

Dear Lisa,

I didn't think my birthday card would elicit such a profound reply! I am so glad to hear that as you gain experience, you are also developing a deeper sense of your calling to the teaching profession. Yes, your reference to Moses was very appropriate. I, for one, am absolutely positive that God has called you to be a teacher. He has given you plenty of gifts and talents for teaching. What's more, the Lord has supplied you with an abundance of interests: a love for the kids, excitement about the subject matter, and a desire to make a difference in the lives of your students. It's as you say, Lisa: You are well on the way!

About the times when you feel overwhelmed: Yes, I know what you mean. All teachers experience these ups and downs. Glad to hear that office consciousness helps you cope. And don't forget to praise the Lord when you're on the upswing again!

Dad

May 19

Hi Dad,

I want to write a bit more about this professionalism thing. Even though I know all this stuff about office and calling and

Kingdom of God, the truth is that in the nitty-gritty of teaching professionalism gets easily squished. Just yesterday, for example, I again got into a spat with one of my colleagues. It was probably my own fault. As you know, I tend to be a bit intense now and then, and not always as diplomatic as I should be. At such times, Dad, I hardly feel like a "fine professional Christian teacher."

Remember our talk about professionalism when I was home for Christmas? I was upset. On the last day before the break one of my colleagues had spouted forth in the teachers' lounge, grinding one of our struggling students into the dirt and blabbing out a confidentiality, something only he and I knew.

Such behavior really made me mad. It's so sad to see Christian teachers badmouthing children and each other. You and I agreed: breaking trust and confidentiality, gossiping, and infighting behind people's backs virtually bring all professional growth to a complete standstill.

Don't get me wrong, Dad! I don't mean to suggest that I'm a professional and my colleagues are not. I could give you a list of examples of my own lack of professionalism. I lose my temper with my kids sometimes, and too often I don't really listen to them as closely as I should.

Now I realize that there is much more to professionalism than issues of confidentiality and classroom moods. I remember a professor in college who at the end of the course gave us a list of characteristics of a professional Christian teacher. Confidentiality was one of them. But he also emphasized competence and professional growth. Teacher competencies included a deep concern for kids, an understanding of how children learn, a thorough grasp of subject matter, good classroom management skills, a wide-ranging repertoire of teaching strategies, and a consistent, all-embracing Christian philosophy of education.

Now it seems to me, Dad, that we can demonstrate these competencies and still not really be a professional. It is how we view these competencies that makes the difference, right? At this point we could easily become very unprofessional. We could become complacent and say: "Hey, I love kids, I know my stuff, and I can handle my class. I've got it together! I have reached my goal. There's nothing left for me to learn." That sort of complacency gets us quickly stuck in a rut, right? It soon turns us into competent fossils!

But Dad, I don't want to become a competent fossil! That's why I see myself as on the way to becoming a fine professional Christian teacher. I know you see yourself that way, too, even after more than 30 years of teaching. We never really arrive. Seeing ourselves as "on the way" is in itself a sign of professionalism, don't you think? As soon as we think we have all the answers and can stop learning, we cease to be professional.

Pardon me for sounding judgmental, Dad, but I think that some teachers take professionalism less seriously than they should. Part of the problem is that in many ways schools are places that discourage professionalism. How can we really flourish professionally when we are asked to run ourselves ragged teaching large numbers of children in a limited space of time? When do we really have time to reflect on what we're doing or supposed to do? Time to read, study, and grow?

For that reason I cherish the occasional inservice days. I'm glad that my school provides financial assistance for teachers who want to hone their skills by pursuing advanced degrees. But more needs to be done to encourage true professionalism, don't you think? I want to talk to you about this sometime. I feel that there is so much more we can do to develop schools where not only the staff is professional, but where you literally breathe a professional atmosphere. I want to teach in schools where we encourage each other to grow, where the learning of all children is really our primary concern, where we *work as a team, and where discipleship is clearly up front everywhere in our program.*

Well, I guess I'm dreaming a bit, Dad! But I think you know what I mean.

Time to run!

Love,
Lisa

Thursday, May 24

Dear Lisa,

I love your dream about the truly professional Christian school. Do you mind if I dream along with you? Here goes: You walk into such a fine professional school and you immediately sense that the teachers are dedicated to their teaching task *and* to professional growth. In the staff lounge you see a variety of recent professional journals, obviously wrinkled and read. On the calendar in the staff room you see weekly meetings in which the teachers report on seminars they have taken or conferences they attended. Such reports include planned applications to their own classrooms. There is also a schedule of class visits: every teacher in the school gets time off periodically to visit other classrooms and observe the teachers teach. Such visits are followed by discussion and debriefing. Several teachers have volunteered to have their teaching activities videotaped to be shown and discussed at regular staff meetings.

In this school the teachers are assigned to small cluster groups which allow them to discuss personal problems and problems with students. Curriculum committees systematically review the school's program, conduct research, and prepare proposals. These proposals include time frames, suggested steps for implementation, and means of evaluation.

Throughout the school there is a sense of devotion to the Lord, to the students, and to each other. Much time is set aside for prayer. Servanthood and discipleship are practiced and modeled. The entire school is a collaborative community. Kitchen staff, custodians, and bus drivers are consulted and participate in school planning. Especially important are the regularly scheduled sessions in which the entire staff, sometimes with student representatives present, focus on the overarching mission of the school. At such sessions the goals are rearticulated and reevaluated. Pertinent questions are posed: How are we doing in this school? Is our curriculum meeting the goal? Do our instructional practices reflect our mission? What about the way we evaluate our students or the way in which we build and maintain community? How does our professional growth fit into the larger task of the school? What kind of professionalism is appropriate for our school?

The parents and the board are heavily involved in all these professional activities. Volunteers, aides, and substitutes are ready to step in at a moment's notice. The board makes sure that there is time and money available. . . .

Ah, are we dreaming? We live in an imperfect world. The stumbling blocks and obstacles are many. Professionalism, too, is often elusive and sometimes an illusion. Nevertheless, let's agree once again that we must keep before us the difference between what *is* the case and what *ought to be* the case. We are talking about this big word "normativity" again—normativity understood in a Christian way: not what people set up as norms and standards, but what the Lord requires. Ultimately, professionalism (it's about time we define the word!) means that we continually seek to discern God's will for the special task to which the Lord has appointed us. It means that we profess the truth and testify to the Author of the Truth as we guide, unfold, and enable our children into the ways of knowledgeable and competent discipleship. Not easy! Yet, it is what we must strive to do.

I will end this scribble by adapting an insight I learned from Calvin Seerveld many years ago. It goes something like this: If the Lord were to return today and walk into our school, what would he ask us? Would he ask, "Are you a perfectly professional Christian teacher? Is this school completely and thoroughly professional in all its ways?" No, he probably would not ask these questions, because he knows our situation. In fact, he knows our situation so well that he died for it. That is why he would probably ask—even demand: "But are you *working* at it?"

Let's keep working at it!

Dad

NOTES